# EPSTEIN-BARR VIRUS

## My Journey and Winning the Fight

# EPSTEIN-BARR VIRUS

## My Journey and WINNING THE FIGHT

BY

TRISTINA H. BOWN

www.bookstandpublishing.com

Published by
Bookstand Publishing
Pasadena, CA 91101
4842_3



ISBN 978-1-953710-18-5

## ACKNOWLEDGEMENTS

Thank you to my family for seeing me through this journey of Epstein-Barr virus and being so kind and understanding. Thank you to my husband for writing about what families go through. Thank you to Tom Haroldsen, my editor for pushing me to continue to write this book and believing in my ability to help other people along their own journey in healing. Thank you to Joe Williamsen for creating a beautiful cover and the graphic design. Thank you to God for giving me the strength to stay strong through this journey and continuing to bless me with so many blessings. God bless you all with this virus as it takes a true courageous hero to endure to the end with Epstein-Barr virus.

# FOREWORD

This is my journey and recipe for getting well over a wicked virus that most people will come into contact with sometime in their life. Not everyone reacts to this virus the same. Some people will have an immune system that will be able to ward this off and a lot of us will have an immune system that is tired and worn out because we have been burning the candle at both ends. We have basically created a perfect storm in our bodies for this virus to totally erupt and change our lives forever. Please join me in my journey and recipe for getting better and fighting the battle to put this little nightmare into remission once and for all. This is a life changing journey for sure.

# TABLE OF CONTENTS

# Chapter 1
# HOW IT BEGAN

My story starts about the year of 1983. I was living in a double-wide trailer in North Salt Lake, Utah, with my first husband. I had my first little boy with me and he was only 3 years old. I had just received a laparoscopy the day before at our local hospital. I got up and started our day with cereal and cartoons. As I was fixing my son his cereal and also my own breakfast, a wave of panic and a feeling like I was going to pass out came over me. Not knowing what was going on, I called 911 and asked them to please come and get me. I was very concerned for my son and was not quite sure what was wrong with me, other than I felt like I was going to pass out. As they arrived, one by one the paramedics asked me what I had been taking. I kept reassuring the medics that I had not taken anything. I am not a drug addict and had just had surgery the day before.

So off we went to a local hospital with my little boy with us. I was in a cold sweat and just was not feeling like myself. I had never had that kind of feeling before. I just assumed it might have been from the surgery and anesthesia. As I was laying in the ER, the nurses were giving my son a popsicle. My grandmother later showed up and told the doctor and nurses that it was a hypoglycemic attack as it runs in our family. I was still feeling a little confused and not sure what to think of it all.

My blood results came back which showed that I had a kidney infection. My glucose was in the normal range, and so I was released and sent home. I know the paramedics were happy to see there were no narcotics in my system, which of course I already knew.

So that was the start of what became a spiral down effect of my health and life. It was one thing after another. I started getting up at night throwing up and being extremely nauseated. I could not be left alone. I continued to have panic attacks on a day-to-day basis. I was always nervous and full of anxiety. I was beginning to think my life was over and that I had a very serious health condition. Thank heavens for my grandmother, as she just continued to take me to the doctors every other day. My doctor was beginning to become quite frustrated with me. Everything in my blood test seemed to look normal. He didn't seem to believe it, but I knew something was wrong. Very wrong.

My health continued to decline. I was unable to eat almost anything, as I would throw it right back up. I could not function nor could I live as a normal person. I had been working at a veterinary clinic at the time and had to cut my hours back to two days a week. My husband was in construction and just continued to work wondering if his wife was a hypochondriac.

After numerous tests and a process of elimination, including checking me for MS, Lupus, and a number of autoimmune diseases, my doctor concluded that I had a severe virus and I might not get better for six months. At the time I was sick, EBV was not very well known and had just barely been introduced into the medical field. My husband at the time was quite a heavy drinker and I did have a psychiatrist tell me that I was a co-dependent of his alcoholism. The psychiatrist told me I should be hospitalized so my husband could see how sick he was making me.

I was told several times to "snap out of it," and to quit putting so much stress and pressure on my husband. My husband one time did tell me he thought I was a hypochondriac. I had lost a lot of weight and was always nervous and full of anxiety. My heartbeat was always extremely rapid. I tried anxiety prescriptions but nothing helped. I could not go to the store or even really leave my home. I felt so trapped in what seemed to be a very nervous unhealthy body. I was homebound with no energy and unable to calm this over-active body that felt like I was constantly on an adrenaline overload. I was still living in and out of the ER for months. I did become friends with one of the ER doctors who was really concerned about my anxiety. He was not sure what to do with me but kept trying me on different anti-anxiety medications. I continued to eat a horrible diet not knowing what to do or how to live. At the time I felt like I was literally just existing. I had no support from anyone, nor did I have any information on the wicked virus that I would soon learn was plaguing me.

My doctor sent me home with no information or any instructions to give me direction. Thank heavens for my grandmother as she started to treat me for hypoglycemia. It runs in our family. She has always lived on a strict diet to curve her disease and following her regimen did help a little bit. My grandmother talked the doctor into putting me on Librium. It is a nerve pill and she thought it might help me. My mind continued to be more cloudy, and I felt like I was in a bubble constantly. I could not handle any stress at all, or it would send my adrenals into an uproar and I felt as though I was having a nervous breakdown. I also continued to have panic and or anxiety attacks if left alone. I still was not showing any signs of getting better. With my mother living out of the country in Japan and my husband working out of town as well, it was determined that I should move in with my grandmother. I still could not be left alone. If I tried to do anything my heart would just start to beat rapidly and I felt like I was ready to pass out.

It was not too bad living with my grandmother as she did get me on a strict diet and started to give me a few supplements. More than anything, she got me to start taking some good vitamins. As time went on, I would go back to my double wide to stay with my husband on the weekends. It was hard but I was determined that I would get better and live a normal life. I later found out that my babysitter was diagnosed with EBV and of course we shared drinks when I would get home from work.

I became pregnant after eight months of living back and forth between my grandmother's home and ours, and knew I needed to move home. So I packed up my little boy and we moved home. My husband's work landed a construction job locally so that made it easier for me to stay at home. My neighbors were really good to me and started to invite me on walks. I would push my son in the stroller, and we would really take some long walks. I did start to feel better, but I could tell I was not completely myself. I was not watching my diet very well and was always dizzy and had vertigo. When I would take walks and come home, my head would spin and I usually would have to sit down for the rest of the day.

I still could not concentrate and had a hard time accomplishing a small task but did give it my best. I always felt like I was spinning my wheels and not getting anywhere. I never felt like I was living a quality life but knew my son needed me. After the birth of my second son, I started to feel even worse. I had no energy and could hardly function but again did my best. This virus never really hit my throat or lymph nodes in my neck; mine was always in my stomach and throughout my body. I felt constantly like I had the worst flu or virus you could ever have with no relief. I would go to bed with it and wake up with it. It became my companion and I felt like I was constantly walking on eggs shells not to wake it up. It also caused me to have horrible nightmares.

I never really took any kinds of medications for the symptoms--I just peddled through it. I guess I was always too afraid that I would have side effects from it and with the way that I felt, I know I did not want to feel any worse.

With my marriage in a turmoil and realizing I had married an alcoholic, I knew that to save myself and my sons I needed to get out and move to a new place. That was a difficult decision, as I knew I would have to depend on myself now and would not have any help. It was apparent though that my husband was not going to change until he got help and I simply could not be that person to help him. So I found a condo near some of my relatives and packed myself up and moved out. I thought I would die. With my adrenals being so taxed and literally in overdrive, I to this day have no idea how I made it through the moving process. But my journey with EBV was just beginning.

# Chapter 2

# HYPOGLYCEMIA OR EBV?

After moving into a condominium with my two boys, I noticed how closely related this virus was to hypoglycemia. I had been tested for gestational diabetes when I was pregnant with my first son. I had the 6-hour glucose tolerance test done by my gynecologist. My glucose curve was all over the place with a high of 146 and then down to 45 within an hour. I thought I would pass out before the test was done.

Since I was diagnosed with EBV I noticed even worse glucose swings and wondered if the virus played a big role in me having hypoglycemia, or did the EBV just exacerbate it? It seemed like everything I ate would give me symptoms of low blood sugar, or I would swing the other way and be very thirsty and then would crash and feel like I needed to lay down.

I would have to carry food with me wherever I went. If my stomach got the least bit empty, I would start to shake as if I had not eaten for hours. It was really getting to be ridiculous. I was known as the girl who always carried a can of refried beans with her!

The wonderful thing about living with a grandmother is both the support that you need and the understanding--especially with someone else who has hypoglycemia. She has battled hypoglycemia throughout her life. When you are a child and cannot understand why your grandmother is shaking and needs food now and does in fact get better after eating something, it all makes sense when you are older and now get to experience the same disease.

Something else I experienced along with hypoglycemia was having my gallbladder removed. I had a normal diet, or should I say for a 21-year-old my diet was normal. But of course I didn't eat well, as I did divulge in a lot of carbs and sugar. However, after my gallbladder was removed within a year it seemed my hypoglycemia got worse. I was once told by a doctor that when you have an organ removed, for instance your gallbladder, that it puts added extra stress on the surrounding organs. So your liver, pancreas and stomach are all in the vicinity of where your gallbladder is.

One thing that I did notice was phantom pains. It seemed that with my gallbladder gone, I was having pains as if my gallbladder was still there. This I heard from my own doctor is common. Nevertheless, I was not having any main gallbladder attacks and did not have any more crystals that were forming in my gallbladder. But I noticed my digestion was beginning to be a little more disturbed than normal. The doctors don't tell you about the side effects of getting your gallbladder out. I had no idea and I now know a few other friends and family that have experienced the same symptoms.

I also believe that this was not such a great surgery for the Epstein-Barr Virus and could have even added to the symptoms. Whenever you have any kind of an upset to your body such as surgery, it will add stress to your system and just one more malady to your list of recovery.

On top of the surgery, you now have hypoglycemia as your body is trying to balance out. What a mess. Believe me, you sometimes feel like you are nothing but a walking disaster. Nothing seems to work properly and now you are having glucose swings that are even harder to regulate than the up and down swings of Epstein-Barr Virus. By now though, thanks to my grandmother, I was beginning to understand what was going on with my body and why the swings of my glucose were getting so bad.

Number one was my diet and number two was the stress I was under living with an alcoholic. Something desperately needed to be done and I needed to make some drastic changes immediately.

Another interesting aspect of hypoglycemia is how the symptoms mimic those symptoms of Epstein-Barr Virus. I would like to name a few. Hopefully these are most of them:

- Allergies to cvcrything
- Anxiety
- Apathy
- Back aches
- Blurred vision
- Brain fog
- Constant sore throats
- Crying spells
- Depression
- Digestion disturbances
- Headaches and migraines
- Heart palpitations
- Heavy periods for females
- Hot flashes
- Jaw aches
- Joint pain

- Lack of sex drive for males
- Neck aches
- Numbness and tingling all over
- Panic attacks
- Ringing in the ears
- Seclusion
- Sensitivity to light and sounds
- Severe fatigue
- Severe hunger in between meals
- Shakiness
- Suicide thoughts
- Swollen Liver
- Swollen lymph glands
- Thyroid problems
- Unable to concentrate
- Unable to sleep
- Vertigo
- Very anti-social

# Chapter 3

# WHAT IS EPSTEIN-BARR VIRUS AND WHERE DID IT COME FROM?

In my research, I found that Epstein-Barr Virus was discovered in March of 1964. The Lancet Medical Journal published an article of research from three scientists called Anthony Epstein, Yvonne Barr, and Burt Achong. They had discovered the first human virus that can cause cancer. This was a little mind- boggling for me and I researched further to find out that the cancers that Epstein-Barr Virus can increase your risk of nasopharyngeal cancer, which is cancer of the sinus located in the back of the nose. It also can cause certain types of fast-growing lymphomas such as Burkitts Lymphoma. It could even be linked to Hodgkins-Lymphoma and some cases of stomach cancer.

Well by now I was really concerned as this virus was affecting my digestive system and lymph nodes around my stomach. Stomach cancer and colon cancer run in my family and I have lost two grandparents with these types of cancers. I knew my risk would be increased having Epstein-Barr Virus. So now what? I had read an article about Burkitts Lymphoma which was named after a doctor who had discovered the cancer in 1985. The discovery was made by Dr. Dennis Burkitts in Ugandan children. Since then several breakthroughs and discoveries have been made including Epstein-Barr Virus and its connection. Epstein-Barr is actually considered a herpes virus and can cause shingles, cold sores, and of course the herpes outbreak.

What I began wondering is how all of these are related? Burkitts Lymphoma can also be caused from Malaria which is a virus spread by mosquitos. One thought that I had might be that these viruses simply weaken the immune system, allowing infected B-cells to change into cancer cells. Apparently, Epstein-Barr Virus is quite common and everyone comes into contact with it at some point of their life. It is spread through bodily fluids such as saliva and is looking for the perfect host with the perfect storm and compromised immune system. I came in contact with it from a babysitter who was watching my children. We had been sharing a drink and I had no idea she had been diagnosed with the dreadful virus.

I believe why some of us get hit with it so hard is this: In our world today our bodies, souls and spirits get hit with stress from every direction. We fall short of a good diet, plenty of sleep, exercise and an all-around healthy life. I also believe certain genes that we inherit can determine whether our immune systems can withstand life's challenges. All of us have tendencies to get laxed in our daily lives and routines and fall into bad habits caring for ourselves. Self-care is so extremely important in today's world.

My grandmother died of stomach cancer in 1990 after a long battle of chemotherapy with no surgery. When she passed away, they performed an autopsy on her and determined that the stomach cancer she had was not common in the U.S. but common in Asia, a nation where their diet consists of a lot of smoked ham. I remember my grandmother eating smoked ham faithfully for years with a piece of homemade bran/wheat bread and one fried egg on top of the piece of ham. She made this bread once a week to supply her with her breakfast. My grandmother also suffered from hypoglycemia which made it difficult for her to fast or skip meals. She would also carry around food with her in case of her sugar levels dropping. She passed away at the age of 69 which is still quite young. I wonder now if she might not have had Epstein-Barr Virus. I look back at her life and when I lived with her, and she seemed to have a lot of similar symptoms like I had. She experienced a lot of fatigue on a day-to-day basis and would have a lot of brain fog with depression and muscle aches. She slept in a neck brace because of migraine headaches and could not sleep in a normal bed but she had to sleep sitting up. My mother now has had mono twice and shows similar symptoms of Epstein-Barr Virus but has never been officially tested for it. My son has also had mono and tests very positive for Epstein-Barr Virus. I had Epstein-Barr Virus when I was pregnant with him and I know it is carried over in the blood.

# Chapter 4

# EBV AND CONNECTION WITH HYPOGLYCEMIA, CHRONIC FATIGUE AND FIBROMYALGIA

Let's first break down each of these diseases. Hypoglycemia is of course low blood sugar. When I was pregnant with my first son my gynecologist recommended that I have a 6-hour glucose tolerance test. This would inform them if I was pre-determined for diabetes or had gestational diabetes. You first go into the lab fasting and they draw a sample of blood. Then the lab technician gives you a small glass of what seemed to me to be straight sugar. Then every half an hour the lab draws a sample of blood to see how your body reacts to the large amount of sugar you have just been given. It also lets the lab know how your pancreas is functioning and if your body is regulating your insulin levels with the large amount of sugar you have just been given.

At the end of the test I thought I was going to pass out. I was shaky and very sweaty. During the very last vile of blood that was drawn I had food in one hand while they were drawing blood from my other arm. My test results came back very positive for gestational diabetes and also hypoglycemia. Gestational diabetes simply means that when a woman is pregnant, the placental hormones can cause high blood sugar levels. The women that develop gestational diabetes are at higher risk of developing type 2 diabetes later in life.

My sugar level went from 85 with the first draw to 149 after the glass of glucose and back down to almost 52 within half an hour. My doctor told me that if your level drops below fasting level then you have hypoglycemia. If your glucose level gets above 110 during the test then you are considered pre-diabetic. I was testing positive for both.

The next step my doctor had me do was speak with a dietician. She instructed me on diet and said if I stay away from sweets and a lot of carbohydrates then I should be able to live a healthy life. She also instructed me that if I were to start eating a lot of junk and sugar that I am very predisposed to type 2 diabetes. So I started to eat, what I thought of at the time, was a good diet. Later I would find out that diet was not at all that good.

On one last note—a lot of people have been misled to believe is that if you have hypoglycemia which is low blood sugar, then you do need sugar, which is very far from the truth. What is happening in your body is your pancreas is producing too much insulin. So what would happen if you ate more sugar? Yes, your body would continue to produce even more insulin. The way to get your sugar regulated is to eat a high protein diet so that your pancreas is not being overtaxed. Everything you eat eventually turns to glucose in your system, so the trick is to bring up your glucose slowly. If you bring it up too fast your body will just continue to have sugar swings and believe me that is not fun at all. It effects your body, mind and soul.

Now let's talk about fibromyalgia. Fibromyalgia, believe it or not, can be accompanied by fatigue and altered sleep, memory and mood. It requires a medical diagnosis and is basically a process of illumination. There are no specific imaging or lab tests for this disease. Arthritis and infections can raise your chance of getting fibromyalgia. Fibromyalgia cannot be cured, so the medical field says. It is a disorder caused by widespread musculoskeletal pain accompanied by fatigue, sleep, and of course the memory and mood issues. It also causes extreme inflammation of the fibers in your soft tissue.

Fibromyalgia can be treated though with success. In my many years of studying Epstein-Barr Virus, I can tell you that 99.9 % of us all have symptoms of fibromyalgia. I also believe that PTSD caused from either childhood trauma or even adult trauma can activate symptoms of fibromyalgia. I have also seen that a person suffering from a either a long-term illness or virus can also have the symptoms of fibromyalgia. I have read that fibromyalgia amplifies painful sensations by affecting the way your brain processes pain signals. Whether they be emotional pain or physical pain. I thought this was quite interesting learning about fibromyalgia. I was also told, by my doctor, that fibromyalgia is simply a symptom of something deeper rooted going on. In other words, please see your doctor and get extensive blood work done and imaging to determine whether you have fibromyalgia or if there might not be another disease lurking in your body somewhere.

Now for Chronic Fatigue—it is also referred to as myalgic encephalomyelitis, characterized by long-term fatigue and other persistent symptoms that limit a person's ability to carry out normal daily activities. Epstein-Barr Virus will cause this particular symptom and is quite common among people suffering with the virus. There is no cure for it and it also can be caused from genetic, biological, infectious and psychological mechanisms. It seems to run more rampant with women than with men. This could be because of hormonal fluctuations and disturbances due to birth control. Some people see absolutely no relief when they have slept or rested for days or even weeks.

When people have lost a loved one or are going through a grieving process, they can also suffer with a lot of fatigue. Loss of a job or divorce or even a change in a job can cause a lot of fatigue. Sometimes the flu can cause severe fatigue or even a major surgery. Usually, it does clear up after a period of time. But sometimes it doesn't clear up when you think it should and can carry on for months. This is the time that maybe some hidden disease or illness can be the cause. Doctors usually perform a process of elimination to determine the cause. It could be as simple as being low on one of your chemicals in your body such as thyroid or it could be as serious as heart trouble.

Epstein-Barr Virus has also been called chronic fatigue because the person cannot seem to function as a normal human being without having to lay down, take naps or simply sleep the rest of the day. I believe that your body is working so hard to repair itself and overcome the virus that is just exhausts you. I have been to point of sheer exhaustion and fallen asleep very easily, only to be awakened by a panic feeling and a racing heart. I am not really sure where that came from other than my adrenal glands being over exhausted or taxed. As I have read a lot of other stories from sufferers this seems to be common after you have been asleep for quite some time. Also, after you feel so fatigued and feel like garbage after you have just had a 2-hour nap it is almost impossible to fall asleep at night. Your body simply feels like it could rest for days and your mind will not shut down. This disease is another one that has no cure or a set test to diagnose it. It, again, is a disorder that has discovered through a process of elimination.

I do know from my own personal journey that proper diet and nutrition with some exercise seems to lessen the symptoms. Also, counseling with a good counselor can help you organize your thoughts and days. I also believe that your brain can use as much help as your body to help you heal. I will discuss a lot of this in the upcoming chapters on what to do for yourself and how I helped myself to heal.

We have now discussed 3 disorders that Epstein-Barr Virus can cause and if you are already plagued with any of these, Epstein-Barr will not only make them worse but will magnify them one thousand times. I personally suffered with them but not so much the fibromyalgia until later when I became in my 40s, and then I really suffered with symptoms like it but did not realize what it was. I had a lot of severe neck aches and lower back aches. I did not have bad headaches unless I ate something that was irritating to my body or I might have had a slight allergy to like Vitamin C. If I ate any food that contained a lot of Vitamin C, I would end up with a pretty bad headache. I did not suffer with migraines like a lot of other sufferers have.

Epstein-Barr causes all three of these diseases or symptoms to these diseases. Hypoglycemia can already be in place and if you are having a flare up with EBV the symptoms, again, are magnified. All three of these diseases are also very devastating and are magnified when suffering from EBV. Epstein-Barr sufferers are always suffering with different ailments that affect the mind, body and soul. It is a very devastating and wicked virus. From one day to the next, you never know what you will be suffering with.

When you wake in the morning it is really a toss of the coin as to whether you will even be able to crawl out of bed. Sometimes you can tell that if you have a little depression in your brain that morning, there is a likely chance that the rest of your body doesn't feel very good. The first thing that has to happen is usually a visit to the kitchen to find something to eat. You're so weak but yet you know that food and nutrition is the first thought on your mind and weak body. That is usually because your glucose is low in your body and you feel shaky.

Another symptom of hypoglycemia. After you have eaten something to hopefully get the shakes gone away you notice your body aches and you can hardly move because of tightness and soreness in your muscles. Then the fatigue sets in and you really feel like it is time to go back to bed. Thinking of getting in the shower sounds exhausting and trying to do anything productive sounds extremely exhausting. By now you are so fatigued that making it back to bed is merely impossible, so you hit the couch to lay down immediately. This is chronic fatigue creeping up on you.

# Chapter 5

# HOW EPSTEIN-BARR AFFECTS THE LIVER AND DIGESTION

I have talked a lot about different symptoms that sufferers have with this dreadful virus, but now I would like to talk about how this virus effects the digestive system and liver.

My first symptom of Epstein-Barr Virus was vomiting. Every night for weeks, I would get up in the middle of the night and vomit. I wasn't really nauseated but could not keep anything down. After that I would go back to bed and feel dizzy and fatigued. I always felt as if a stomach flu was coming on but never really erupted. I did that for weeks and throughout the day would have horrible stomach cramps and bloating. At that time, I never really thought much of it other than my stomach hurt. I continued to work and eat a poor diet, which consisted of a lot of bread. I would later find out that the bread with the yeast in it was literally feeding the virus.

I wrote a story on Celiac Disease and how it effects the digestive tract and sometimes wondered if celiac was not caused from Epstein-Barr Virus. I have read a lot of studies that in fact say a lot of the diseases we now have start in the gut. I thought that was quite interesting as to how EBV first started to affect me. I also know that celiac disease can be inherited. I also know that my son inherited EBV from me when I was pregnant with him. So who knows how all of this gets started? The more I study about viruses and illnesses and diseases, the more I learn that there is so much that science does not know. The good thing is that they are continuing to study these things out every day.

Epstein-Barr Virus can actually cause a mild self-limited hepatitis. I know that as a sufferer my liver always felt swollen as did my spleen. It does affect both these organs. People suffering with mono have severe digestion problems, stomach cramps and inflamed livers as well as spleens. When my son was in 6th grade, his teacher called me and said "I think your son has ADD." I asked why she thought this and she said "because he stares out the window all of the time, rests his head on the desk and never finishes his work." Well of course being a mother I headed straight over to the school and pulled him out. I did sit him down and asked him if he felt okay and he told me that he did not feel good and that his throat hurt all the time, as did his stomach. So we headed to the doctor to see what was wrong with him. I had a sneaking suspicion what was going on but wanted some blood tests to make sure.

The first thing that the PA said was that he probably was suffering from acid reflux, and that is why his throat hurt all of the time and why his stomach was sore as well. I said okay but will you please just test him for Epstein-Barr and mono. The PA agreed to take some blood and have him tested. Well I can tell you that the results were just as I had suspected. He was positive for both EBV and mono.

We pulled him out of school and put him on bed rest. We also pulled him from any sports so he would not get hit in the gut. Yes, his spleen was enlarged and that is where the soreness in his stomach was coming from. His liver enzymes were normal, but his liver was also a little inflamed. He stayed home for a few months and then started to show signs of recovering. Before long he wanted to go back to school, but I can tell you that I had a long talk with his teacher, and during recess he was to rest and lay down. He took a blanket and a pillow so he would be comfortable. It seems like when he started into junior high he was doing excellently. We had him involved in a few sports including baseball where he was the main pitcher.

Now for me, it wasn't that easy and took me a lot longer time to recovery. Through the different flare ups of the virus I guess my liver decided to develop what is now called a fatty liver. My liver enzymes are always normal so that is a good thing. I am always accused of being a heavy alcohol drinker, though I don't drink at all and haven't for over 30 years. I am not a diabetic which can also cause a fatty liver. I am also not obese and again have never been overweight other than when I was pregnant, and all for a good reason. I don't eat a lot of fatty foods and eat a very clean diet. So where did the Fatty Liver come from?

One of my doctors that is educated on EBV told me that my liver has developed fat cells around it to protect it from the virus. Mono and Epstein-Barr really attack the liver, so I guess it is safe to say that the liver might have a mind of its own and knows how to protect itself. There is no cure for it other than to avoid alcohol, eat a very well-balanced diet, control your diabetes and of course exercise. So that is exactly what I do. I have not had an MRI recently to determine how my liver is doing but I do have my blood tests done to determine how my triglycerides are doing as well as my liver enzymes. There is medication that can be taken to keep your levels at a healthy place. I personally have never taken any of these medications and hopefully never will. I do take a few herbs for the liver in hopes that this will help with keeping my liver healthy. I will discuss this in another chapter.

At one point in my life and with another flare up of this virus, I honestly thought I had stomach cancer. Stomach cancer runs in my family as well as colon cancer and I could not seem to live a normal life; my stomach hurt so bad and was so acidy all of the time. I also had continuous loose stools and symptoms of IBS. I remember going through a large bottle of Pepto Bismol once a week. I know that wasn't good for me but it did give me a little relief sometimes. I would keep it next to my bed so I could take it through the night just to get some sort of sleep. I was miserable for about six months with nausea and pain. That is when I went in for an MRI and when they found the fatty liver. Apparently, it had nothing to do with my symptoms because my blood work was very normal.

I finally started to feel a little better after six months. I started on some heavy doses of probiotics. That really did start to help with pain, nausea and bloating. When you have a virus taxing your immune system it throws everything off in your system, including the bacteria count in your stomach. There is good bacteria and bad bacteria. When you have been on antibiotics for a long period of time it throws off your bacteria count and causes the bad bacteria to grow and kill of the good bacteria. It also causes another disorder called candida, which I was very full of as well. If you have ever seen someone's tongue that is completely white, chances are they are full of candida. There also could be other diseases and disorders that can cause a lot of white coating to the tongue. This is what happens as a result of taking antibiotics for a long period of time. In females it usually causes yeast infections of the genitals.

I also had to go off all breads. The yeast in the bread would cause my stomach to bloat and cramp up. I did start to notice a big change in the way my stomach felt, and I did not wake up to a acidy anxious stomach.

# Chapter 6

# DEPRESSION AND EPSTEIN-BARR VIRUS

I remember living out in the countryside in New Mexico. We lived on a horse ranch about 40 miles from the nearest town which was Roswell. It was me, my Mom, little brother and stepdad. We also had several workers from Mexico that did a lot of the duties around the barns, cleaning stalls and breaking horses.

The horse ranch we lived on was in the Hondo Valley just east of Ruidosa Downs, where the famous horse races were always held. We raised Arabians and Polo Ponies for one of the most-wealthy men in the United States and the largest landowner in New Mexico. Each summer there would be polo games at the ranch and me and my best friend Renae would hot walk the polo ponies after they had played a match. Horses have to be walked to cool down slowly or they can develop colic and twist their intestines. You never want your horse to develop that because it means a visit to the veterinarian or a house call, which could turn out to be very devastating and the loss of a horse. So the hot walkers, which we were called, had a very important job involving the game of polo. We always had so much fun and of course made a little money.

Renae would usually stay the weekend with me and go home on Sunday to return to Roswell, where she lived and went to school. I went to school at Hondo High in the valley I lived in, so we never did attend school together. I would always dread when Sunday would roll around because I knew that meant she would be leaving. After she would leave I would have the most horrible waves of sadness. I felt so lonesome and lost when she would go. Almost a type of depression for days until I could see a light at the end of the tunnel for her to return the next weekend.

That was my first time I had ever felt some sort of sadness and depression from life. But nothing would ever prepare me for the depression that I would get from a virus.

I know that Epstein-Barr can cause lesions on the brain and I am not quite sure that plays a big role in the depression that follows having a flare up of the virus. I never did have lesions on my brain that I know of, but I sure felt at times that I did. My brain never did work quite as well after I contracted Epstein-Barr Virus.

I can tell you that besides all of the horrible wicked physical symptoms that you experience, that the depression and brain fog you develop is almost worse than the physical symptoms. When you don't have at least your brain functioning, you feel like you have nothing left. It is hard enough trying to exist with the physical symptoms, but then to add the brain fog and depression, that can just about be a little too much. You feel like if you can do anything to at least feel normal in your brain, then you have accomplished it all.

One thing that sometimes helped me was to journal all of my thoughts. If you could get at least a few negative thoughts out of your brain, then that would allow your brain to maybe heal and at least give it some strength to heal your body. Even if I didn't feel very good one day I would at least write some thoughts on what I had accomplished that day so I could see some progress or give me hope. Some of the things that I would write down would include if I even took a shower, made our bed, brushed my teeth or even put on some makeup. I was homebound for close to five years, so anything I accomplished that day was huge.

I also noticed that every time I would have a flare up of the virus, it seemed like when I would get over the physical symptoms, the last place it would travel would be to my brain. I swear sometimes I thought this virus had a mind of its own or was basically alive. It would travel to a different location every day. But when it landed in my brain, it was devastatingly wicked. It was almost like I knew what it would be like to feel normal but thought I would never have my brain back again.

I was known as the girl that sat in the window and stared outside. I would sit in the box seat of the window of our bedroom and stare for hours looking at the outside world. I would really try and envision myself as being well and running or walking and enjoying the outdoors. I thought if I envisioned myself as being well long enough then maybe someday it would come true.

Speaking of the outdoors, I have to mention a story about how healing the sun and outdoors can be. When we would take trips to Florida, I always remember I just didn't feel good and trying to remember why we were going in the first place. My parents and brothers all lived there and we would visit them frequently. One reason was to check on my parents and the other was because we love the ocean and beaches so much on the Gulf side.

I lived in Florida once for about two years growing up in the military with my Dad being in the Air Force. So we moved every two years. It wasn't fun but made me very tough and independent. I am not sure if that was all that good when it came time to getting married, but nevertheless moving a lot got into my blood stream and I do love traveling. But again, every time we would travel, I would think to myself, "I just don't feel good. Why are we doing this again?" And by the way I was usually always the one who made out travel plans and purchased our plane tickets.

While we would visit with either my parents or brothers, we would make it a point of attending the beach several days while we were there. We would set up our chairs and umbrella for my husband while I basked in the sun and worked on my tan. It wasn't just a few hours but for most of the day. We also would float out onto the ocean and really enjoy the sea water. I had always heard that the sea water can be very therapeutic, almost like soaking in an Epson salt bath. Most of the time the ocean would be pretty warm as well, so it really felt like therapeutic. Throughout the week I would struggle a little but start to feel a little better each day. When it was time to leave for home, I would have this overwhelming burst of energy and feel so good even mentally. We would fly home and for weeks I would be burning the candle at both ends again and have an over abundant schedule. I think that is why a lot of us end up with EBV because we just don't know how to slow down.

I realized that besides soaking in the ocean, sitting in the sun and relaxing in a beach chair, I was in fact healing myself inside and out. I also read a lot of books at this time. Usually they were self-help books. Not only did I read but I also caught up on my journal.

The sun is a very healing element in our lives. Everyone seems to do better during the summer because of its healing agents. Not only does it give us a lot of vitamin D but it also regulates the Serotonin in our brains. Serotonin is our happy hormone which helps with our stress levels, and when that is out of balance it can throw us a curve and throw every chemical in our body off. I do suffer with SAD during the winter months and it does get worse as I get older, so for me the sun is almost a must.

Of course there are other faculties that can cause our brains to be out of whack and out of balance. Environment plays a particularly big role in our mental state. We live by a refinery that has a lot of extra waste and exhaust blowing out of it stacks and the smell is really horrible at times. I can't begin to tell you how many times the smell has woken me up out of a dead sleep and how panicked my body would feel. I would have a hangover feeling in my head and feel shaky in my body. Our physical bodies can a lot of times predict how our brains function. I know that after working with people with EBV, they have come to find out that through their blood work some of their vitamins or minerals can be off and cause mental disturbances in their brains. Potassium, Vitamin D, Calcium and our B-12 and other vitamins can cause a lot of unpleasant side effects in our brain. I have also experienced myself the effects of food allergies. Can you imagine all of the poor teachers that get sent all these children that have just had a big bowl of sugar-coated cereal? These poor children are running on such a big sugar high for about 2-3 hours and then have a fast drop in their glucose. I can't imagine being a teacher and having 26-30 students crashing all at once and trying to teach them as well. We wonder why children are having such a hard time in school or why all of these shootings and bullying are getting so much more common. When I was in school, I could never imagine acting or experiencing the things in school that are now happening. Suicide is now sky rocketing and addiction no matter what it is, which now there are so many new addictions including electronics, are now completely out of control.

The fluctuation of our hormones can certainly control our mental state and moods. I finally started to keep track of my moods during the month. I realized that when I was in my menstruating years I would go through a deep depression and just have a feeling of being "off" for about a week after that last day of my menstruation cycle. I also realized that this was because my hormone level would drop quite rapidly during that week. Estrogen and progesterone levels get to their highest levels that they can get to right before you begin your menstruation cycle and then drop rapidly when you are done menstruating. I really fought my emotions and mental state during this time and would just remember that it would soon pass.

Some women have to go on hormone replacement medications. My doctor did try to get me to at least try some hormone replacement because it got so bad, but I decided against it and wanted to see if my body would balance itself out on its own. I did fight the battle and I can tell you that EBV definitely makes a woman's menstruation 100 times worse. Every little detail of having a menstruation cycle is magnified when you are suffering from EBV. I also know that for a woman who has just had a baby and is now going through the baby blues or postpartum depression, she has a significant drop in her hormones. It is, to say the least, very devastating when it comes to the fluctuation of female and male hormones.

Now for men, after speaking to many through my years of study on this virus, they suffer from lack of sex drive which woman also suffer from, and can also suffer symptoms from a low level of male hormones. I also know after speaking to my husband several times, who also suffers with mild EBV thanks to me, that men go through mood swings and can go through a male menopause. There are times when a man, through blood work results, will have to go on hormone replacement therapy as a result of a low testosterone. Epstein-Barr Virus literally can cause a fluctuation of every single vitamin, mineral and chemical in your body. So when you are suffering with EBV, please know that you are not going crazy. When one chemical is off it makes the rest of them simply fluctuate out of control. When Epstein-Barr has a flare up, virtually every chemical is thrown off its normal level throughout your body and the feeling that results is very devastating.

Let me mention one more detail of a certain organ and its function within the body. That would be the thyroid and its connection to Epstein-Barr Virus. It simple doesn't function and can become sluggish. Whenever I would have my blood work performed by a lab and my doctor would go over the results with me, my thyroid levels would be low. They would be in the normal range but in the low normal range. My doctor would recommend a thyroid replacement, but I would always decline. I felt like my body would balance itself out eventually. EBV can also cause hyperthyroidism. This can be very devastating. Your body feels like it is on uber drive and like you have been given some sort of dose of steroid.

This disease is also known as Hashimotos and is another autoimmune disease. I didn't ever acquire Hashimotos Disease, thank heavens, but do know that EBV and Hashimotos can run hand in hand as they are both autoimmune diseases. I think EBV makes the thyroid think that is it is the cause of all the symptoms caused from EBV and then makes the thyroid sick itself. Then what happens is the body tries to reject it and that makes it sluggish and stop performing its job. You do have to have your thyroid, but if you have had yours removed as a result of cancer, then you will be put on thyroxin, a thyroid hormone replacement.

I had a friend whose thyroid had cancer and did have to have it removed. I believe she also suffered from EBV. Sometimes she would start to feel so good that she would quit taking her thyroxin. This was not a good situation and she would suffer horribly with anxiety and weight loss as well as deep depression as a result of not taking her thyroxin medication. She realized that she would never be able to quit taking her thyroid medication. So I do know how important your thyroid is and how well it helps to maintain and balance out our hormones which we have throughout our bodies. It is actually very critical to stay on your thyroid hormone, especially in the case where you have had it removed.

I also think that having an endocrinologist on board is extremely important in helping maintain or at least trying to maintain a balanced endocrine system. Personally, I did not ever get one for myself as I would just have my doctor keep track of my chemical levels and vitamins in my blood work. If I continued to get any worse than what I was, I certainly would have brought an endocrinologist on board. I was told at one point that maybe it would be a good idea to seek one out but never did.

I wished sometimes I could just say to depression, "please go away and leave me alone as you are really bothering me," but it is simply just not that easy. It is a process and I know that is why I journal a lot. It helps release the brain from added extra stress that it does not need to hang onto. I have been to several continuing education seminars in dealing with the brain and what I have found out through personal experience and education is that your brain does need a break. It can't continue to function properly and not have any type of a break or even a type of therapy. So journaling is what I have found out that can give your brain that break it needs. If you will simply journal your thoughts and daily tasks it will release your brain from the burden of carrying any worries around. It simply gives your brain a break and allows it to move forward and not dwell on the past. Your brain at all times needs to be cleaned out. Our brains have a little filing cabinet in the back and can store up all types of negative events unfortunately. So, in order to clean it up we must journal to put those thoughts and events on paper so they cannot burden us or our brain any further. That will give your brain a chance to concentrate on the virus and help to heal our bodies.

Another important aspect in my recovery of depression was having a relationship with God. I also thought about our Savior Jesus Christ and how he suffered and felt every one of our aliments including mental ailments. He suffered and died for us and I cannot even imagine what that was like. I would find myself sleeping with my scriptures under my pillow for any kind of comfort. There were nights when I went to sleep not knowing if I would wake up and the scriptures gave me comfort. I would attend my faith of church that I grew up in on a regular basis to give me hope in enduring to the end.

My faith in my Savior Jesus Christ is sometimes the only concept that kept me going. I did pray fervently day and night. Sometimes at night I would wake up and feel so horrible and to the point of not knowing if I could go on. It was at that time that I would pray with every strength I had left in me to please let me know if I was to continue moving on and I would undoubtedly get an overwhelming feeling to please hang in there, as this will all pass and it is only temporary. I would a lot of times feel guardian angels surround me and try to give me the strength I needed to even get up in the morning or try and find something positive about the day.

I have worked with people who have let their past life control their current life and watch the devastation they put themselves through. If they could only learn to forgive and journal, they could be freed from the bonds of unforgiving tendencies. They could be freed from the bonds of the past and be able to look to the future with hope, happiness and embracing the new upcoming days with positive outlooks. It isn't hard but it does take dedication and discipline to write every night. Both my husband and I journal every night. Every once in a while I will be too tired that night and put off my journaling but the next day I would pull out my journal and continue to write and catch up. It is quite empowering and rewarding and eventually you will see how well your brain can heal itself with less stress weighing it down.

# Chapter 7

# LIVING WITH EPSTEIN-BARR AND YOUR FAMILY

This chapter is meant to explain and let your family know that you still love them no matter how discouraged they might get with you while you are healing. This chapter is also a must for your family to read. It will better explain what you are going through, what to expect and above all, to please have patience.

When I was married to my first husband and when I contacted Epstein-Barr, there didn't seem to be much information on the virus. My grandmother would take me up to my doctor's office about three times a week. Every trip I would pray that first of all I would make it up there and second of all my doctor would miraculously figure out what was going on with me, and finally have a name for the illness I was experiencing. I literally thought I was dying and felt like it as well.

Like I have mentioned before, it took my doctor six months to determine what was wrong with me through process of elimination and he still never put a label on my condition. He only told me that I had a really bad virus and I might not feel very good can't for six months. Well, try 25 years with five more flare ups. There was no information about this virus and at the time there was not even a name for it. It wasn't until

10 years after that, that there was even a real test for EBV. Now there are several different titer tests for EBV.

If you would have looked at me you would have thought, "I have no idea why she just can't snap out of it and get well. She looks perfectly fine to me." This is a statement I heard constantly, especially from my ex-husband and his friends. No matter what I did I just didn't feel good and could barely function. It almost got to the point where I needed care around the clock and had to have help with my first son at the time. I could not be left alone because of the anxiety and depression and of course the all-around feeling like you are dying. It was so frustrating to me and I know that it was really frustrating to family friends. At one point a lot of my friends thought I was doing it for attention. Some even labeled me as a hypochondriac. My ex-husband used to go out and drink and everything else that goes along with drinking and at the time his friends thought I was doing it so he would stay home with me and not go out and have fun. I know now that my marriage was not a healthy one to begin with.

My thoughts on this are if you do have a family member that has been diagnosed with EBV or Mono or any other auto immune illness, that if they say they don't feel good, chances are they don't feel good. My sons also questioned my health issues, but since I have recovered and now am back to normal and my Type A self again, they realize they were wrong and that I really was sick. They both are dealing with depression and anxiety that they have found out can almost be debilitating. My friends and family have also realized that you don't have to be in a wheelchair or a cast or have a big bandage around your head with crutches to be sick. Illnesses can come in all shapes and forms and sizes literally. Just because someone looks great on the outside does not mean they are not hurting on the inside and that they might not be suffering from an illness that is completely putting their life on hold.

My first husband never ever once went to the doctor with me. He was never told by a professional that, yes, I was sick, but they weren't sure what it was. He only went off of what I told him that my doctor had said, and I know that a lot of times he thought I was making it all up. My grandmother knew there was something wrong with me because my whole demeaner was different and I was not this cute little happy-go-lucky girl anymore. I don't even remember laughing at all during this time. It was all I could do to get through the day.

Another frustrating aspect of EBV is how long it takes you to get better or even feeling halfway like a normal person. I know that did frustrate my grandmother as well. When people get the flu, you just go to bed and drink liquids for a few days and take some Tylenol or aspirin or ibuprofen or whatever your choice is of over the counter drugs and you're well in 5-7 days. Not with EBV. This little virus hangs on for months and for the most part can hang on for years.

Now with all of this being said, can you imagine how your poor family must feel after about 12 months of showing no improvements. I know that because of its debilitating symptoms, marriages are hard to survive as well as any relationship. Please trust me as a survivor. I would have cut my right arm off to get well and be done with it. It just simply was not that easy. When you marry, you marry for better for worse, for richer or poor. So, I pray that most of you have a solid marriage before this ever hits any one of you. This will be a very challenging trial for any marriage—good or rocky.

My husband now was a God send for me when I had a reactivation with this virus. We had just gotten married and he had an accident riding my mountain bike coming down off a mountain. He fractured his wrist and clavicle and had two surgeries to plate and screw the bones back together. I took care of him and the household, our kids and our small stone business. With being in a new marriage we were challenged with combining families. He had his father and brother living with him at the time and I had two little boys. The stress took its toll on me and after he recovered, I crashed and burned. I was not eating well at the time and really had not been educated on supplements or diet. I had not been educated on anything. So, I went to the Internet which wasn't very big at the time and started to read anything I could get my brain around. I did find a book that was written on chronic fatigue with information on EBV. The book really did help me and started to enlighten me about what exactly I was dealing with and how to recover. When I went to a different doctor and had my EBV titer levels checked, my doctor took one look at me and asked how I was even functioning. The book I was reading talked about a man who was quite ill and his EBV titer levels were about 2600. Mine were over 3200. My doctor did say that my levels were higher than anyone he had ever seen. Thank heavens we now had a label and some sort of a level of where my titer levels were and where they should be.

The tests for EBV are now a lot different. They test for early and current antigens. One antigen might be your IgG level which is immunoglobulin G. It is a type of antibody. It is the most common type of antibody found in blood circulation. IgG molecules are created and released by Plasma B cells. These are cells that will show up if you have had EBV for quite some time. They show that you have had flare ups of EBV in the past. Now IgM are the antibodies that show up when you are first infected with a new bacteria or germ. They are your body's first line of defense against any infections of any sort relating to flus and viruses. These viruses can include hepatitis, Mono, rheumatoid arthritis, kidney damage, parasite infection or even multiple sclerosis. And yes, EBV mimics a lot of the same symptoms that multiple sclerosis causes like lesions on the brain. That is why it might take your doctor several weeks to determine exactly what is causing you to be so sick. He will perform process of illumination with several blood tests, EKGs, x-rays, and biopsies if necessary,

I am going to let my husband who I have been married to now for almost 28 years make some comments and inserts on what it is like to be married to a spouse with EBV. I know that it is very frustrating and hard to endure this trial, but it can also help in a lot of ways cement your family relationship better in any way whether you are married or not. Your whole household gets turned upside down and all of a sudden Plan B has to be put into place. Almost like if a major disaster just struck your home, life or marriage because this is basically what has just happened. This can also be a trial for any family whether you are with a partner, a daughter or son who has just been diagnosed with it or single by yourself and have to move home because you can no longer work and care for yourself. It is a life altering experience and has to be taken with patience and lots of love and understanding. Believe me I am not putting it lightly that there has to be love and understanding. It would not hurt to bring in a counselor for understanding a chronic illness. Most counselors are very educated on chronic illnesses, especially EBV. They can certainly help with the stress that comes with a chronic illness. The last thing that anybody enduring this virus needs is to have a lot of stress because of ignorance and impatience.

# Chapter 8

# HEARING FROM A SPOUSE'S PERSPECTIVE OF EBV

I am the author's husband of 28 years and my sweetheart has asked that I contribute to this work by adding my perspective, the perspective of the spouse of someone afflicted with the Epstein-Barr Virus. Incidentally I also have been diagnosed with the virus. I have had episodes of being fatigued and not feeling good for the last 20 years but have never had it debilitate me like it has my wife.

While I'm honored and happy to take on this task, I can say I find it greatly intimidating, but I believe my perspective may be of some benefit and utility to those in a similar position, and that is the only aim I have as I pen this contribution.

Tristina and I were introduced by our next-door neighbor who was also a very close friend of my wife. We were of course single at the time, both veterans of failed first marriages interested in getting on with life and all the wonder it has to offer.

We hit it off immediately and felt a strong connection almost instantly. Of course I was stunned by her beauty, but what I felt right off the bat was that there was nothing average about this girl, she was special in the most profound meaning of the term.

Outwardly, physically, she appeared to me as the very perfect picture of health and vitality; great skin, gorgeous hair, and her bright blue eyes were mesmerizing. Her musculature was exceptional as well—I mean she was "Buff" as they say. We dated for just a few months before deciding to get on with it and get married. A grand bonus to me was the fact that she had two sons, and as I had not been able to have children of my own, I saw this as a great blessing and opportunity in my life which it was and continues to be to this day.

At first, I never "suspected" she was dealing with a most debilitating foe as is Epstein-Barr. She seemed to be up for anything I suggested such as hikes and walks and all types of outdoor activities that were physically demanding. Her attitude was always totally upbeat and positive. Little did I know how hard of a struggle it was for her back then.

I remember the first inkling I got that there may be something wrong was during a trip we took to Seattle while we were dating to introduce me to her mother. One day we decided to go to the beach and do some beach combing, which was definitely one of mine, and her, favorite things to do. As we arrived at a particular beach that her mother suggested we explore, I took off like I always do and noticed that after an hour of trotting, running, climbing over rocks and through foliage that Tristina was having a hard time keeping up with me. I almost wondered if she was hanging back to spend time with her mother but later learned she simply did not have the energy.

At some point I decided to go back and join them in their less frenetic pace, maybe I'd even enjoy it. I guess voices carry on a long empty beach because I remember that I was quite a distance from them as I overheard her mom kind of scolding her about “blowing it with this guy” by becoming aware of her “condition.” What? What was she talking about? I heard something about some “chronic fatigue” or something as I got closer. This is where I can see sometimes that families just don’t “Get It” or understand. You look great so just “Get over It,” which is so far from the truth of what the person is feeling and experiencing and going through. It doesn’t work that way. I found out later when I was diagnosed with it how sick it can make you feel and that rest alone doesn’t make you get better all of a sudden. It takes a lot of time and especially understanding from you spouses, parents, families, friends and co-workers.

Tristina had mentioned to me that she often got tired sooner than she liked and that she had a non-fatal virus that caused this premature tiring or fatigue. Like a typical self-centered guy I hardly listened then, but now my interest was somewhat peaked. I didn’t bring it up then, but thought I’d inquire of her at some later point when we were back in Utah.

We discussed it more in depth upon our return home. I wasn’t obsessed, I just wanted to know a little more about it and when I concluded that it wasn’t fatal, I more or less lost interest. We were having so much fun and enjoying our togetherness that I wasn’t bothered by it quite frankly. I mean she looked so great on the outside and was a vivacious mother of two great boys who actually liked me and enjoyed being with me. Talk about me not blowing it. Again I had no idea how hard she was struggling on the inside. She certainly hid it well.

We were married in the month of December and everything seemed to be just fine through the winter. Occasionally she brought the boys to some of my job sites which I thoroughly enjoyed. The following spring, I was injured in a bicycle accident. My left clavicle was obliterated and had to be platted with 8 screws in order for it to heal correctly. At first everything seemed fine. She was the best "nurse" a man could ever hope for, but as the days and weeks passed where I was really no help at all around the house, I noticed her really start to drag.

As my health improved hers really started to decline precipitously. I was pretty much back to normal by late summer and it was a good thing I was because Tristina had really been forced to slow down. I was greatly troubled because I'd never had experience with a physical malady that had little to no outward signatures. Her color was good, she was still beautiful, and she really had no high fevers, etc. I really wondered what in the world was going on.

I was raised where we didn't see a doctor unless we were bleeding to death or there was a bone sticking out where it wasn't supposed to be. This was new to me and I was puzzled and I have to admit here that I was somewhat suspicious of what was actually going on. I thought maybe she had shut down mentally as a result of having to pull the weight of the family solo for some many months with no help at all and trying to take care of me who can rather be a big boob when injured. She was blaming her condition on a so called "virus" that neither I nor anyone else had ever heard of. I had heard of hypochondria and I wondered if that was what we were dealing with. I never knew what to expect and how this virus actually affects your mind, spirit and soul.

Her condition only worsened until she was practically bedridden. This was about the third or fourth time this had happened according to Tristina. As a husband I just took over where she left off with the many roles that were completely foreign to me such as cooking and otherwise preparing meals and doing all the cleaning.

Tristina started actively experimenting with nutrition and I remember that no matter how bad she felt or how tired she was or how tired and fatigued she was, she would still clean the house or help me with cooking or running my business. She even put an article in our local paper and started a support group with other sufferers as herself that had been diagnosed with Epstein-Barr Virus. I also remember going to the doctor with her to have her EBV titers checked and listening to the doctor tell her that he had never seen anyone with such high EBV titers and also explained that he could understand why she was feeling the way she did. This was the turning point that really started to make me re-think what was happening to my wife.

It was very obvious that she hated her condition and what it was doing to her. She would always refer to it as the "wicked monster." I watched her force herself to get up and walk around our house and do laps in the kitchen and living room. I could definitely see that a physical effort was required to even think of recovering from this "wicked monster." I had been a highly trained athlete for much of my youth and recognized the signs of authentic physical effort and exertion. I saw it in her as she fought whatever this was tooth and nail. She was clearly not "sand-bagging." She had the grim determination of any Olympic athlete you can think of.

Some days she would feel better than others and some weeks better than others but she never gave up on her diet, supplements, studies and a detailed will to not give up and kick this thing once and for all. Some minutes and hours were actually better than others but she was still in a state of general physical debilitation. I came to understand that what she was enduring was a reactivation or flare up of that dreadful virus. She informed me that it was rather cyclical. It would go into remission for periods of a time and then it would come back with a vengeance upon having a lot of stress at once. There was never any warning or way to tell when the virus did come back how bad the activation would be or how long it would last.

I guess the one word that would sum up the emotions spawned in the spouse or family member with EBV would be total frustration. But then it is ridiculous to attempt to summarize those emotions with just one word. I felt many negative emotions as a result of what I saw as the trial of my wife's life—more particularly the trial of our marriage and lives. There were many emotions that we dealt with like confusion, sorrow, depression, anxiety, nervousness, futility, impatience, self-pity (why me, why us?), pessimism, anger, and of course resentment. I resented the universe and or God or whatever there was to resent for allowing this to happen to her and to us.

I was frustrated at how our home was basically turned upside down and how everything had to be adjusted. Also how some things just had to be dropped from consideration like all the fun things we used to do. Camping, hiking, taking walks and all the fun outside activities were completely put on hold. It was impossible to show my true frustration outwardly, however, because the only real victim in the entire scenario never acted like a victim. I really felt ridiculous any time I was tempted to vocalize my frustration. I just continued to watch her struggle and bottled it up inside of me and carried on with life. Her example made the whole experience tolerable.

Through this all I have come to recognize that Tristina is an amazing individual with unbounded courage and tenacity. She is also fiercely independent, which was one of the most difficult aspects of her condition, to be such a "doer" and yet for extended periods of time be unable to "do" neither for herself or anyone else.

The boys didn't know what to think. I thing the summarizing term for both of them would be confusion for sure. As most of us know kids aren't the most patient and understanding of the human family. They are all about themselves as they navigate life. They have to be in the early going mode of survival and can only think of themselves I have come to understand. Now the youngest son was also diagnosed with Epstein-Barr and Mono when he was in 6th grade and continues to suffer with reactivation and flare ups into his 30s, so he is a little more to understand the effects that it has had on his mother. When they were younger though the little ones were quite contrarians when it came to understanding what was wrong with their mother. Their constant skepticism only added to the battle, especially when you couldn't blame them at the time. When something is unknown to kids and they see their mother suffering with no outward symptoms, it is quite impossible to deal with.

I marveled as I watched how innovative Tristina was and how that innovation was the product of a "never say never" or "never say die" attitude with regards to the Epstein-Barr Virus. I was in awe as she constantly and consistently working, searching, and implementing different strategies to combat this demon.

Despite all the negative aspects of the virus, we actually had a pretty positive vibe in our home. This again was because Tristina refused to give-in or be defeated by it.

This all-in attitude is what led her to consistently experiment with nutrition and supplements and exercise. She was relentless. The right combination of which has ultimately led to her present condition of extremely long-term remission.

In summary then, I would say crazily enough, that for me it has been a net positive experience because I've been witness to the indomitable human spirit. I have seen that it is possible to outwit this virus and actually beat it into submission if one is truly dedicated to that task. I've witnessed what can be accomplished through shear, raw discipline. Though it seemed like for Tristina, it was akin to running in quicksand, she never gave up or stopped moving through her journey of healing.

It's next to impossible for me to crab and complain about this and that minor malady I might have to endure after being a witness to what she has overcome.

I feel blessed to have been able to witness that truly, very little in this life is impossible. Tenacity is the key I believe and also a very strong will to survive and win. We have to be tenacious at all times and go on the attack against life and its diseases. When we remain in the defensive position, that of going back on our heels, it is very easy to get toppled. If we are in a forward leaning attack position, it is much more difficult for that which we battle to knock us backward.

My wife has truly led us on this journey of discovery and I know that what she has accomplished is unfortunately not the norm, but for any who truly desire to get and stay on top of the EBV I doubt there is anyone better prepared to in that desire and accomplishment. She has a wealth of knowledge not just of the virus itself, but how to defeat it in a long term. She is also at all times ready, willing and able to help others however, wherever and whenever she can. She continues to run circles around me and our boys and now 8 grandchildren. She has to stay well to keep up with them and work her many jobs she has including caring for other people in her health care profession. She is truly a treasure.

# Chapter 9

# FORGIVENESS IS A MUST

This is a tough subject because everyone of us has a reason not to forgive, but I must say it is a must to forgive when you are in our position and carrying around this dreadful virus. Believe it or not emotions can feed illnesses, and carrying around a grudge can indeed keep you sick.

Through our domestication we continue to "fill our cups" with daily emotional garbage. I know it doesn't seem like garbage, but if it isn't any type of a subject that is going to better our situation, then it is garbage.

Gossip, backstabbing, lying, or basically being "thrown under the bus" constitutes drivel. In my life I have realized that it is not worth being hung up on others causing us pain and frustration because of a statement they have made or some type of act they have committed towards us.

It adds fuel to our already taxed and compromised immune system. This was a decision I had to make and stick with if I was to get well. I had a pretty good childhood and didn't start to experience self- destruction with someone you love until I married my first husband who ended up being an alcoholic. Addiction is a tough one and when you are involved in a relationship with someone who is an addict, life can get really interestingly tough. Not only are you fighting addiction but you are also fighting your own feelings of toxic shame.

I remember always covering for my ex-husband and on the other hand sticking up for him, which is in turn enabling him as well. The exhaustion and sleepless nights I would go through wondering if he would come home and what condition he would come home in. It played havoc on my health for sure. I lost a lot of weight and this was the exact time that I contacted Epstein-Barr Virus. I really went through a lot of bitterness and anger towards him. I realized I had to forgive as soon as I could. I remember visiting with a religious leader and continued to share with him my experiences of being married to him. He told me to write him a letter. I did just that and it was a lengthy letter, but I wrote all my feelings down and how his alcoholism had destroyed our family and especially my life. Then my religious leader told me that we could burn it together. He explained to me that it would leave us in smoke and rise towards the heavens. There are enough angels that will take over my feelings and emotions and it would help me heal spiritually, physically, and emotionally. I actually did this exercise several times.

Another way that I helped myself to learn to forgive was getting EMDR counseling-eye movement desensitization reprocessing. What a wonderful counseling modality. Not only does it help you to move forward and not be stuck in the past but it also helps your brain reset its thinking. What a marvelous way to move forward and clear your brain.

I was taught journaling at a very young age. At the time we called our journals diaries. I always kept one and continued to write in it almost every day. To this day I continue to write in what is now my journal. Even when I was my sickest and almost bedridden for years, I still continued to write in my journal. What I would write about wouldn't be how my day went because at the time it was not going well and I always felt crappy. So I decided to write down every single thing that I accomplished that day-from taking a bath to saying my prayers and putting on some make up. If I made it down stairs and fixed my own lunch or washed a dish, I would write it down. The most amazing and interesting outlook on all that I did is how the list would get longer and I would feel encouraged to do more. Obviously as I continued to heal my list got longer which was again very encouraging to me.

When the United States and all the world experienced 911, I marveled at how the country came together. The day after was a very sobering day for all of us. Our feelings were a bit terrified, to say the least, not knowing what had just happened and wondering if we were due for more disasters and tragedy. Everyone was helping each other and their seemed to be a lot of compassion as well as love in the air for one another. Big things that everyone used to focus on and let ruin our days became small little grains of sand that soon became minuet in our existence. The words "Thank You" became the new words and "I love you" became a new phrase that didn't seem hard to express any more.

Forgiveness was becoming a new way of life. After all we had just witnessed acts from people that probably had no idea what they were actually doing, I mean who would in their right mind and witnessed thousands of innocent people lose their lives and become disabled for the rest of their lives. We didn't have a choice but to forgive and move on so we could progress and get through this tragedy together. Our churches were now full to the brim and Sundays became a must to recognize God, learn how to pray and worship our Savior all over again.

Remember the Grinch who stole Christmas? I believe he must have been abused as a youth and carried so much anger around that he wanted the whole Whoville village to suffer and not have Christmas. While the Grinch was stealing presents, he runs into sweet little Cindy Lou. This was a trigger point in the Grinch's life where his heart started to soften and the anger lines in his face actually start to fade as he finds love and kindness shown to him by this sweet little girl after he had just lied to her and told her he was fixing their Christmas tree when he was really stealing all their presents.

So after his heart softens, and he realizes that Christmas is not about presents and money but maybe about compassion and forgiveness of a person who might have just been dealt a rough hand at life. The whole townspeople of Whoville forgive the Grinch and show him how to celebrate Christmas with love and empathy. I really love this movie and it is fun to watch the transition in the Grinch as Cindy Lou, just one little person from Whoville, shows some great love toward this monster about to ruin their Christmas.

Now I am not saying to go out and live life completely without being aware of our surroundings and just live as if you have nothing to worry about and be oblivious to the world. By all means be aware of people who will come into your life that might be suffering from their own crisis and try and pass it on as I always say. It is okay to dismiss what I call "Toxic People." They will be everywhere in our lives and can come in friendly forms as well as family forms. This does not mean that you have to submit yourself to any sort of abuse. If you are unaware if you might be submitting yourself to abuse then please call a hot line as there are many out there that can help you through an abusive relationship and also get you the help you need.

There is no room in our lives right now for abuse and relationships that are toxic while trying to heal from a horrific virus. There is of course just daily life that we deal with like raising families, paying bills and trying to hold down a job. Co-workers can also be rough on you while you are healing because they simply don't understand. I mean after all you look fine so just "get over it," right?

I worked at a veterinary clinic for seven years and after being injured with my shoulder and having to be relocated to the office while healing, I discovered the practice manager had been embezzling. I was not surprised but now had proof as to what was taking place and why we all were not getting raises as well as having cut backs. About the time that I was ready to blow the whistle, I was laid off from my job because of course of cutbacks. I was quite surprised as it was announced in a meeting and was not confirmed to me. This took me a very long time to move forward and forgive the owner and veterinarian as well as the office manager who continued to work there for years. Even though my job was offered back to me after realizing what was going on, I did not want to submit myself to a toxic environment again.

As I have said before, forgiveness is a very large emotion that has to be followed through with. If we do not forgive, we are only injuring ourselves and prolonging the need we so desperately need to heal. Forgiveness is an internal process just like grieving. It can take some time but the faster you work towards forgiving then the faster you can progress, move forward and heal.

Let me now just touch on PTSD. This is a probably another real tough aspect of our life and can come in a lot of different forms. It doesn't just affect war veterans coming home from wars and suffering from watching the horrific tragedies that they are submitted to on a day to day basis, which coming from a family of military people I have the utmost respect, love and compassion towards our war veterans and would never disregard their hard work in our behalf. But PTSD can affect all of us at one point or another.

My counselor suffered from an ankle shatter while rock climbing and developed PTSD. My older son passed a kidney stone while camping and had to be rushed to an ER in the middle of nowhere and suffers now with PTSD. Anyone who has been violated either from someone stealing from them or stealing any type of modest personal belonging can suffer from PTSD. Betrayal trauma can cause significant PTSD. Car accidents, first responders, police officers, doctors, nurses, losing a loved one or friend, suicide, addiction, watching an accident or even witnessing someone who is really sick can all cause suffering and bring on PTSD. It can happen at any time in your life and when it does and the emotions are too overwhelming, please get some professional help. I wished I would have had all the tools that are now available to us this day back when I was suffering, as it would have made recovery possibly a lot quicker.

I am now known as the "Duck" that lets those raindrops just flow right off of my back. Each day is a new day to learn and practice forgiveness. I give welcome to every trial that I have as it is only making me stronger and become the best person that I can. The brain needs a break from life as well as your body and eventually will send emotions to a weak spot in your body. This is when a chronic pain can start to set in believe it or not. Not that chronic pain is not a real problem but I have seen with my own eyes and from personal experience can testify that if you are having an emotion from any type of emotional pain, it is a must to get it addressed and taken care of so that it doesn't attach itself to a weak place in your body and become a constant chronic pain.

# Chapter 10

# DIET, SUPPLEMENTS AND EXERCISE

Before I start this chapter on the process of healing, let's talk for a moment on testing for EBV. There are a lot of tests to be done and it is good for you to check where you are with it. There will be the IGG test and also the IGM test. One will be to check to see if there is a current activation and the other will be to check to see if you have had it in the past. There are so many different blood levels that can be checked, so here is the site to help you determine where you are: www.cdc.gov/epstein-barr.

For me personally, I would check once and then go from there. I always just go off of how I feel. For instance, my levels right now are around 175 to 225, and in the past they have been as high as 750. I feel great now with them being around 175 to 225, probably because my body has adapted to my EBV. I wouldn't make a habit of continuing to check your levels only because our brains can sometimes confuse us, and I have to say if you are feeling better and have your levels checked and are running high, then your brain can see that number and convince you that you should be feeling worse than you are and then you actually do feel worse. Your EBV levels will fluctuate all week and all year, so please just maybe check your levels twice a year.

In this chapter I will start off by addressing diet and then get into exercise and the importance of it, although I know that it sounds utterly impossible. I will also discuss my own recipe of supplements, diet and exercise that I used for myself through trial and error. Now what works for me might not work for everyone, and what works for someone else might not work for me. I will touch lightly on supplements because I am not a doctor, and if you do have a doctor you are working with, please keep them in the loop of your recovery and use them as a good source of knowing how much to take of certain supplements. Also, if you have a good health food store that you frequent and you feel comfortable with, use them as a source of knowledge. They are not in this line of work if they didn't know about supplements and dosage. But never forget that we are all different and really sensitive to everything right now, so start off slowly.

When I first contacted Epstein-Barr Virus I had no idea of the importance of diet. I ate horribly and drank soda pop on a day-to-day basis. As I began my studies on what it was going to take to get me back to normal I learned a great deal on herbs, supplements and vitamins. One really important supplement that I came across while holding a support group in my home was Blue Green Algae. At the time my brain was all over the place, and talk about depression? It was almost overwhelming and I was completely desperate to say the least. One of our supporters had also been introduced to this product. There are many blue green algae suppliers around, but you must make sure that it is the algae that is harvested out of the Klamath Falls, Oregon Lake. This supplement has Tryptophan in it which is an amino acid and is an excellent source for fighting depression. Blue green algae is at the bottom of the food chain and is also loaded with antioxidants as well as certain vitamins, minerals and amino acids. I began to see a big difference in my moods and energy within 2-3 weeks after taking it. Thank heavens as I was somewhat desperate to say the least, as I know most of all of us are. I will talk more about the supplements to take further in this chapter and outline a supplement recipe to take. There are quite a few that I will recommend and what they are good for in your diet.

The next most important addition to your healing is of course your diet. Now for me I stopped all red meat, dairy, breads, sugar, caffeine, alcohol, and too much fruit is also a concern because of the natural sugar. The key to getting well is starving the virus and allowing your own body to overcome and fight it off.

The reason that I chose to abandon red meat was because with Epstein-Barr Virus comes a lot of digestion and abdominal pain. Red meat adds to those digestion problems and also takes a lot of energy to break down and digest. This digestion process takes away the energy that your body needs to heal itself. So if your body is busy breaking down foods and metabolizing them so your system can absorb the nutrients it needs, then it is taking away a lot of energy your body needs to fight off the virus.

Milk products carry a lot of preservatives and chemicals to make it safe to sell in the stores. If you milk your own cow and make your own butter and cream, then this may be a different situation in continuing milk products. I still chose to stop all milk products because the lactic acid seemed to stir up the acid content in my stomach and throw off the bacteria balance. With that being said, they also caused a lot of digestion problems and stomach cramps that were simply unbearable.

Breads are nothing but starches and turn into sugar quite quickly in your system, and that again will feed the virus. Viruses, flus and cancer completely feed and thrive on sugar, and that is what we are trying to avoid. One of the most important parts of the reasoning behind omitting bread from my diet was because of the yeast. Yeast also can inflame the lining of your gut and cause gastroenteritis which I suffered from for years. When I omitted breads from my stomach, the problems seemed to subside quite a bit. I started using roll ups instead of breads for my lunch meals. Anytime there was bread served, I would use roll ups instead. They come in many forms such as spinach, tomatoes and wheat. Now if you have a gluten intolerance disease then you will have to read labels for non-gluten food products. There are many food companies now producing products without gluten. Restaurants are now offering menus with food allergies and intolerances of gluten. A lot of restaurants also offer dairy free food items.

Sugars have to be stopped in your diet immediately if you plan on, number one, surviving and number two, healing. I can't begin to tell you of all the information I have read on sugars and the toxic power they have over your immune system. On top of the poison that is being fed to our system from sugar it is also causes inflammation throughout our bodies. Our joints, organs, bones and skin, believe it or not, are all being effected by this inflammatory chemical. The average American consumes over 200 lbs. of sugar a year. Our systems are only equipped to consume approximately 5 lbs. of sugar a year. Now we can see why diabetes and obesity is on the rise. I always think of the pioneers and my ancestors who lived off of their land. They grew their own vegetables, grew their own fruit trees, milked their own cows and raised their own beef. If we went back to living the way our ancestors did, I know there would be less disease and obesity in the world. So we must get back to the basics and start over. One thing that I was told by a nutritionist that I often think about is that for every tablespoon of sugar that you put into your body, it shuts down your immune system for 4 hours because that is how long your body takes to absorb the sugar and break it down and excrete it out of your system. So again anything we are putting into our bodies that takes a lot of time to break down is taking energy from our body in fighting off this wicked virus.

On top of what sugar does to your body, can I just tell you what it does to your brain. The main chemical that our brains function off of is glucose. Believe me, when your glucose is off in your body, it will play havoc with your brain. I think most of you know what I am talking about. Lots of hypoglycemia symptoms for sure. I think a lot of the inbalance of your glucose in your brain is the culprit for depression, anxiety and just an overall uneasy feeling. What your brain feels like can be the most unfathomable symptom of the whole Epstein-Barr Virus nightmare. It is so hard to explain this to someone who looks at you and says, “But you look so good.” Of course you look pretty good. You didn’t just have a car accident or fell off of a cliff; you have an illness that affects you internally with not a lot of outside symptoms. I could go on with the effects of sugar. There are so many great books on sugar and how toxic it is to our bodies. It simply feeds every bad disease you can think of, including EBV and cancer. Now knowing that why would we want to continue to feed our bodies sugar?

I know a lot of you are thinking, "Well everything you eat turns to sugar." I agree whol heartedly with that, but the goal is to eat the proper nutritional foods that will be absorbed and turn into glucose "slowly." We will get to that later on in this chapter.

Caffeine of course is a stimulant. There is not much more to say other than people are looking for a quick pick me up and something to give them a little energy to make it through the day. What caffeine does is it stimulates your adrenal glands and gives you a temporary energy surge to help you get through the morning or even day. Then in the long run it exhausts your adrenal glands and then you eventually suffer with adrenal fatigue. There are great studies coming out about caffeine every day and some are good and some are bad. For the normal person, caffeine might never effect you, but for someone with EBV, it is imperative that you follow the guidelines to getting well.

Caffeine is actually quite addictive might I just add. My mother used to drink coffee faithfully until she got into her 70s and then realized it was causing her bowels to react and we couldn't hardly take her anywhere without having to do a wardrobe change. She eventually got herself weaned off of caffeine with some side effects, one being severe headaches, and POW, no more bowel problems. Please remember again I am no doctor but have had a lot of experience with diets and nutrition and symptoms of EBV. Some of you might not ever be affected by its side effects and some of us might look at caffeine and be wired all day. It is up to you to decide what you can and can't tolerate. Everyone's symptoms are for the most part the same, but for everyone trying to heal it will be trial and error and a continuing trial basis on what works for you.

I think it is very important to talk a little about artificial sweeteners. Like most Americans we are always looking for some type of food or treat that will satisfy our so called "sweet tooth." That might be possible to a normal person who is not suffering from EBV but for us it is simply not an option. There are so many artificial sweeteners out there that can cause havoc on our systems.

When I was pregnant with my first son, I also developed gestational diabetes. My doctor sent me to a nutritionist who heavily educated me on the effects of sugar and also educated me on substitute sugars. She let me know that as we know saccharine has been known to cause cancer, and to stay clear of that. Aspartame, she told me, was discovered from a scientist who spilled formaldehyde on the counter and after it dried, he tasted it in which it had a sweet taste to it. Well I looked up the story and she was right as to where the sweetener originated from. Might I add that formaldehyde is the chemical they use to embalm your body to preserve it. NO THANK YOU.

Now another common sweetener is sorbitol. I remember watching an episode of Dr. Oz in which a man could not figure out why he was having so much gas and loose stools. Dr. Oz went over his diet and day-to-day intake. Well the poor guy was chewing gum out of control because he didn't want bad breath and what do you think the gum was full of? YES, sorbitol. It is used as a laxative. So basically I have shared three of the most common sugar substitutes and I can't find anything good about them. I was also told by this nutritionist that Nutrisweet causes brain disorders. I unfortunately discovered that one on my own. Never again will I eat something with an artificial sweetener in it.

Stevia is plant based. I have tried different products with this in it and have a lot of similar side effects like sugar. Again some of you might be able to tolerate this sugar substitute, but for me and my system, I just can't.

I almost have a lot of the same side effect symptoms with carbonation. This is another tricky chemical that we HAVE to stay away from. Not only are the side effects grueling on our digestive system but the carbonation can rob our bodies of calcium and also start to form calcified crystals in our systems which eventually turn into kidney stones, gall stones and bladder stones. When my Dad was driving trucks for a living after he retired from the Air Force, he was out on the road when all of a sudden he had the most over powering painful feeling shooting from his lower back to the front of his abdomen. He told me he thought and almost wished he could have died from the pain. After getting the truck pulled over safely and getting an ambulance to come and pick him up, the doctors discovered he was passing a kidney stone and you will never believe what the doctor told him to quit immediately. Yes, carbonated drinks. My Dad stopped them altogether and he quit passing kidney stones.

There are so many fun chemicals that have been put in front of us that can become addictive. They are so luring and quenching to our little taste buds. I know because I love carbonated drinks but they don't love me, and I have realized to stay healthy that it is a must that I stay away from them. I don't just mean while we are trying to heal but STOP at once and forever.

In my book I am simply going to outline what worked for me. I will be very basic in all the information I give to you and then it will be up to you to decide what will work best for your body and its chemistry set up. I also recommend getting a good homeopath involved who can do muscle testing and recommend what your body is either asking for or lacking in. Your body does not lie. I have been to several myself, which some have helped me and others were not so helpful. Through study and prayer and trying different supplements, vitamins, minerals, homeopath products and diet, I have been able to overcome this dreadful disease and get it into remission and live a normal healthy life. I know for some of you that sounds impossible, but it is not.

So the next substance I would illuminate from my diet would be alcohol all together. You can't afford to continue with this substance. EBV sufferers don't have room in their lives and the roller coaster that you will be headed down continuing to partake of this substance into your body. Just remember if you have ever had a hangover and how horrible you felt because of the effects of alcohol, you will think twice. One reason is because the hangover feeling you get from alcohol is the feeling you basically have all the time from EBV. I will say that alcohol is a poison and lowers your glucose in your system and that is why a glass of orange juice in the morning with a hangover is recommended to bring that glucose back up to the normal range. On top of the headache and shakiness and all over horrible feeling, who would want that feeling on top of the Epstein Barr? That would be a disaster that would take days to feel normal. NO THANK YOU.

Let me share with you what I have done as far as supplements and diet to get on top of this and get my health back in order.

Might I say again, this is going to be a simple recipe and I won't suggest the dosage on anything. This will have to be something that you will have to do for yourself and also between your doctor and homeopath or someone at the health food store who is a nutritionist or expert at recommending the proper doses for supplements, vitamins, herbs and antioxidants.

A lot of the labels will also give recommendations of the dosage which I would pay attention to. Do not start off heavy on supplements as your body will not tolerate it. I have found with EBV that the sensitivity that you have will only allow you maybe half of the dose that is recommended, and sometimes less than that because our bodies are so toxic to begin with because of the virus.

Now that you know what I have recommended what not to eat, let me start with the best foods that you should eat. This is what I am currently eating and will do so for the rest of my life. I have cheated a few times especially around the holidays and I pay for it. It's not just a day that I pay for it but sometimes can take several days and even months to recover. I don't have to continue to make that mistake nor do I want to go down that road again and miss out on a lot of life that I can live. I mean seriously, don't we all feel sometimes like we have missed out on so much and wasted so much time being sick. I say enough is enough. AGREED???

For breakfast I eat chicken breast and assorted greens. I have eaten peas and green beans for the most part. I mix them together and eat them all morning. I try not to sit down and just eat it all in one sitting. I find my body does great when I slowly eat and let my body digest it slowly. Then you are not overloading your system with too much food and getting that bloating feeling. The only thing I drink is water. It can be filtered or bottled spring water. I know it sounds boring but it is up to you if you want to get feeling better.

Now eggs are not a good source of nutrition with EBV and the reason is because the eggs can carry virus cells. In labs they actually incubate viruses in eggs. I have discovered that eggs also irritate my stomach. So no eggs and of course no bread. Some people have tried hot cereals such as rolled oats. This is what my husband eats every morning for breakfast. For me this was a lot of carbs and I just didn't feel good. The carbs of course break down into sugars pretty quickly and of course feed the virus. I would also feel bloated. The whole point of diet is to feed your body and starve the virus. REMEMBER, the virus loves starches and carbohydrates.

If you find yourself getting hungry before lunch then cut some celery up and just a few carrots and nuts. You will have to determine what nuts are best for your body. A lot of people unfortunately have allergies to nuts, so check what you can tolerate. I have also read a few times that celery juice is great. I have tried it several times and I admit it does help with inflammation and balancing out your glucose. For me I like to just eat the celery because it helps with digestion as well.

For lunch I would do a roll up with either spinach or tomato. Then I would get chicken and lettuce, spinach or whatever greens you like, or tomatoes. There is a lot of controversy going on about tomatoes. Personally I don't eat them because I have to be very careful with vitamin C and they also have a lot of acid. I could not figure out during the end of the summer why my stomach would burn so badly. Then I realized that this was the time in which I would eat all the fresh tomatoes out of our garden. There has been mention of them being a nighttime vegetable and that they can cause some health issues in the long run. Peppers, cucumbers, broccoli and any other kind of greens that you would want to choose to put into your wrap will work. I use just a tiny bit of salad dressing as well, mostly with olive oil as your mix with the greens and chicken. You can also use fish if you choose to. Cut-up apples are also a good choice to add. You will have to get very creative with your diet and what your body will tolerate. I started off slow and then started adding things that were good and acceptable to my system.

For dinner I would have either a pork chop, chicken breast or piece of fish. I always prepare my food with extra virgin olive oil and bake or cook it over a grill. I would also fix some brown rice with either some steamed mixed vegetables or some sort of squash or yam. Mixed salads are a very good source of nutrients and vitamins that we need as well. After you continue to eat a diet like this, you can slowly add in more things like pastas. There are some great pastas and different sauces that are totally vegetarian. You can also make your own sauces using tomatoes. These are the bare basics and I know sound really boring, but if you want to get better then you will have to follow this diet. It really falls into the category of a Mediterranean diet.

There are a lot of different smoothies that can be made to drink throughout the day with natural greens and fruits purchased at the organic produce section. I do like to juice as well, but again I have to be careful mixing certain fruits with vegetables—especially carrots and apples. My favorite juice is a head of celery cut up, a few small carrots and one cucumber and some spinach. If I just juice carrots and apples, I feel like someone has stuck a knife in my stomach if I mix those two. I also do try and limit my fruits to once or twice a week only because of the natural fructose and the Vitamin C I have to be so careful of. My mother was extremely allergic to Vitamin D and would develop severe headaches and Vitamin C does the same thing to me. With EBV it is so common to have allergies to foods. You can experiment with different herbs added to your smoothies but remember to keep things pretty simple starting off and then as you continue to heal and feel better then slowly add other ingredients.

There are a number of different milks that can be used like almond milk, cashew milk, coconut milk and one of my favorites now is oat milk. Both my husband and I use this one. Stay clear of soy milk. There are 3 different flavors of oat milk including vanilla flavored, plain and some with added sugar which we don't use. I also use this in all my cooking recipes.

I will share a recipe with you for homemade banana pancakes and waffles. Now a lot of you will have gluten allergies so you will have to find gluten-free flour. I use organic unbleached flour. I do not make these very often as they are a starch and full of fructose with the bananas. I also put one egg in them. I have noticed that if I have recipes with eggs they don't seem to bother me. I only use an egg for cooking my waffles and nothing else. I never will not eat them on their own.

**BANANA WAFFLES Recipe**

5 ripened bananas
2 cups of organic flour
2 teaspoons of salt
1 egg
1 tablespoon of olive oil
6 tablespoons of cinnamon

Blend well with mixer and use as waffle batter or pancake batter. I don't usually put anything on them but sometimes I will put a little organic peanut butter on them.

**SUGAR-FREE BROWNIES Recipe**

1 can of drained black beans
2 tablespoonfuls of cinnamon
1 teaspoon salt
¼ cup raw cocoa
2 tablespoons raw honey
2 cut up bananas
1 cup dry quick oats

Mix with a blender and put into 9-inch greased pan. Cook on 350 for 30 minutes. They are delicious and good for you, with the Cocoa being an antioxidant.

These waffles and brownies are what I consider treats if you start to crave a treat, which all of us will do. Your body will crave sweets because the virus is telling you it needs to be fed. Be tough and fight it with nutritious treats like these. I only eat these maybe twice a month. The cinnamon in both recipes is excellent for keeping your glucose balanced, and also it is great for your digestion and keeping your gut healthy.

My meals are very simple but this is what you must do to start out your diet. I have a number of fresh vegetables that I steam including brussel sprouts, cauliflower, broccoli, zucchini and very light on the carrots. Baked yams and squashs are also excellent and a good source of vitamin A. I go very light on potatoes but I do have a half of one sometimes for my dinner or even lunch. Red potatoes are the best and can also be baked or steamed. If you think about our ancestors and what they ate all the time, it included strictly meat, potatoes and breads. Unfortunately because of the EBV we have to step our diet up just a bit. I promise you though you will start to feel better. It might not be in weeks or even months but within a year, you should start to see some results. Remember "Slow and easy does it." Again the key is to keep your body well and feed it but starve the virus. It can be done and you will win this fight.

When eating out you can ask the servers to help you with the menu and also mention your diet restriction. They love to help and can make some great suggestions. Most restaurants have a lot of great plates that have meats that you can tolerate as well as steamed vegetables and usually a potato of some sort, but they are willing to trade food items for something you can eat. I do find restaurants always trying to please the customer and especially if you have diet restrictions. Also, a lot of restaurants are now serving vegan plates or vegetarian plates. I know I have also just ordered a chicken salad with a little oil and vinegar on the side. You will have to get creative but I promise you that if I can do this then you can too.

Now let's talk about supplements. I could spend my whole time on a full book writing about supplements, herbs and vitamins but I will be very general and simple.

The first supplement that I mentioned earlier in this chapter was blue green algae. This is the foremost important supplement. The second important supplement and also something that our guts need to keep the bacteria balanced is a good probiotic. I will say if ever there was a bad night that my stomach was keeping me awake, I would relent to taking a Pepcid. This is an over the counter medication and very safe. It calmed my stomach so I could get some sleep, especially when my stomach would be so acidy and feel like it was on fire. This does eventually clear up. There are several probiotics out there so just find one that a nutritionist will recommend. The most important components to look for in a probiotic are your digestive enzymes like amylase, lipase, and protease. The good ones will always be in the refrigerated area. It is extremely important to keep your gut bacteria balanced because usually you have been on so many antibiotics throughout your life prescribed by your doctor for one reason or another.

Another good liquid that helps heal and balance the gut is distilled aloe vera juice. I cannot begin to tell you how this one chemical and liquid can heal you from your mouth to your bowels. The aloe vera juice will also heal your stomach and gut and help with the acid over abundance. Vitamin A, D, and K are extremely important and I would recommend a separate supplement with these three. Also I would recommend a good all- around multi vitamin that is loaded with Vitamin C. I would also include a separate vitamin C supplement to just give your Vitamin C a boost. A lot of homeopaths suggest a Vitamin C cocktail. These are Vitamin C IV's and should be given by a doctor or even licensed chiropractor who has been trained and is licensed to give these IV's. I have not had one as I am allergic to Vitamin C but have heard they are great and give your immune system a boost for about 3 weeks.

One vitamin that my doctor put me on immediately was a Vitamin B-12 injection. I received them once a week for months and then once a month for about a year. Your B-12 level should be between 600-900 but mine was always around 2600. When your immune system is fighting a virus, your fire is burning double time and a half and needs extra B-12. This is going to help the nervous system, help with depression and also boost your energy level. Every time I receive one it feels like I have just taken an antidepressant naturally. How wonderful would that be? Get a B-12 shot and be able to handle life just a little better. Sounds great to me and I have experienced that. Please check with your doctor and have him monitor you while you are receiving these injections.

You will also need some good immune builders. Now this can be tricky because there are a lot of them out there and I will tell you of the ones that I have used. There are also a lot of great immune building combinations with some great chemicals used only for the immune system. Colloidal Silver, onsillit, Reishi mushroom, astragalus, zinc and beet juice are all really great for the immune system. They all have immune components in them and will help to replenish and keep the immune system healthy.

Speaking of just what exactly is the immune system made of and where is it? The immune system is everywhere throughout our bodies. It is a complex network of cells and proteins that defends the body against infection and or bacterias. It also keeps a record of every germ and microbe that has entered our body and has ever defeated so it can recognize and destroy microbes quickly when entering the body. Some of the suggestions I thought were of course nothing but common sense in keeping a healthy immune system. The list starts as to stop smoking, get plenty of rest, try to avoid stress, heat healthy, maintain a healthy weight, wash your hands often, exercise regularly, and eat a diet high in vegetables and fruits. WOW, pretty much what we already know. Our lives just get out of control and start spinning way too fast and we are looking for quick and easy fixes like fast food. It does catch up with us for sure though.

Other supplements that I highly recommend are turmeric for inflammation, onsilliti to help rebuild injured cells, CoQ-10 for your heart and muscle regeneration and also energy and monolaurin with lysine. What happens with EBV and also Covid-19 is the protein shell surrounding the viral cell is extremely hard for our bodies to break through, so our bodies can overcome and kill the viral cells. The monolaurin breaks down that protein shell so our bodies can do their jobs and overcome the viral cells. The lysine is an excellent supplement for herpes viruses which is what EBV is in the family of. One last supplement that I use is a green drink that I purchase on line. Dr. Tony Odonnell has formulated it and I have spoken with him to get permission and allow myself to tell you about it. I use the natural one and it is called Radiant Greens. It has no gluten, no dairy, no GMO and no wheat. I have been drinking this drink for over 9 years. The website is www.radiantgreens.com . Dr. Tony works with sufferers of all sorts and formulates supplements to help get your body strong enough to overcome the disease.

There are several great green drinks that you can purchase and use. Please read the label for sugar content. I chose this one because it is low in vitamin C and has no sugars other than the ones that come from the vegetables and fruits. I also like this product because it has all of the digestive enzymes in it like amylase, lipase, protease, papain, bromelain, and onsillit. Our guts are in a turmoil right now and we need all the help we can get for digestion. It also has ginkgo biloba, red clover, dandelion and green tea, which is excellent for energy and food for the brain. Once I got this built up in my system, I only use it maybe 3-4 times a weeks.

The most important aspect to remember is you might have to rotate a lot of these supplements and not take every one of them every day. You might want to do half of them three days a week every other day and the other supplements 4 days a week rotated every other day too. The blue green algae and distilled aloe vera juice should be taken every day though. I have had no side effects and it has got to be built up in your system quickly. The immune builders should be taken at least 4-6 times a week.

You will find many companies and supplements that sound great and the advertisement will always tell you that you will be healed and feel great in days or your money back. Please be careful and read labels. It will be a matter of trial and error with your body and let me reiterate that what works for me might not work for you. Also, let me be clear that there is again no quick fix for this temporary nightmare.

Many sufferers have tried CBD oils and swear by them. I did try them for a minute but could not tolerate the carrier coconut oil. My stomach just would not tolerate it so I stopped taking them. There are so many companies that will guarantee their product or give you your money back. If that is the case and you want to try them, then by all means give them a try. But again please be very careful trying new products. I have given you a simple outline of what worked for me and my system was extremely sensitive to everything. A lot of Sunday's, at the end of the week, I would take a break from everything other than my diet. I did have to take a month break from all of the probiotics as it was really effecting my brain and I was feeling off a lot of the time. My brain cleared up the uneasy feeling immediately. So with that being said, remember that your bodies can get overloaded with vitamins, minerals and supplements. So if you need to take a break, then please do it and then start them back up again but maybe at a lower dose and not every day. When we are dealing with a virus, our bodies can feel very toxic and overloading it with a lot of supplements can in fact start a toxic overload. So slow and easy does it.

I did try a few herbs but the herbs that I use are in the green drink that I take; and now that it is built up in my system, again I only take it now about 3-4 times a week. The only herb that I would take in addition is in the form of a tea and that was chamomile tea. I really did like something warm at night that would help me sleep. I also use herbs in oil forms and wear them. I use them instead of perfumes. As a therapist I also use them on my clients and they love them. Not only are they therapeutic but the Ole factory, meaning the nose, can be such a healing modality if the right oils are used. It triggers certain senses in the brain. Odors take a direct route to the limbic system, including the onsilli and the hippocampus, the regions related to emotion and memory. This is why sometimes smells can trigger bad experiences that have happened and also good experiences we have had in our life.

A lot of people express remembering their grandmothers when smelling roses, probably because that was one of the most popular scents back in that era. I use a lot of cinnamon and clove, as that is supposed to help with the immune system and ward off viruses. It's a very happy smell for me because obviously it reminds me of Christmas and the birth of the Savior. I also use orange as that is a happy oil and is supposed to help you with an overall well-being and happiness. Orange makes us feel like we are somewhere warm or in a tropical area. There are a number of blends that I use and wear everyday but you will have to find out what you can tolerate and what you like to smell. Lavender is a popular one and seems to really have a calming effect and an overall feeling of Zen. But I worked with a lot of women that said it gave them headaches. You will have to see what works and smells best for you. You don't have to wear them as I have just felt they help me. A lot of people use them in a diffuser throughout their homes. Please do not use Tea Tree oils if you have pets. They are toxic to pets and can make them extremely sick.

My next most important and foremost healing modality will be exercise. I know a lot of you are probably thinking, are you kidding me, and no, I am not kidding you. I was homebound and bedbound for 5 years and I wished I had known then what I know now. If all you have is the inside of your home then great. Start off slow and do laps in your home. This is what I started to do. The key is to start getting your body really healthy and moving now and be able to get your heart rate up. I mean really, who doesn't want a bunch of endorphins increased in our brain, which is what happens when we increase our circulation and build up our cardio endurance. Walk a few laps in your home every day. Start off with maybe 10 laps. Then move up to 15 and then 20 laps. When you feel good enough, step outside and walk a few laps in your driveway or walk to your mail box. This is what I did for a few months. Circulation and drinking lots of water will get this virus flushed out of your system as well and is a must. If you can get some weights, then start using weights with short, small lifts. Start off slowly again with maybe three reps of 10 twice a day and then continue to increase each week. It is important to start building muscle mass as we have lost a lot of that sitting around while not feeling good. You will actually feel yourself continue to get strong. I was amazed even at my worst how much better I felt even mentally and psychologically. I just felt better that I had accomplished an actual exercise routine.

Eventually I felt good enough to join a gym and really started to get into some heavy exercising. I ran my first 5k race in 2015 and continue to sign up for them. I do cardio for about 40-45 minutes and then lift weights for another 30 minutes. I even swim every chance I get. If I contact a cold or flu of any kind, I seem to come out of it fairly quickly. I have had several extremely stressful situations in my life in which I totally thought I would relapse, and the virus would reactivate, but I am positive now because my body was so physically fit that I was able to survive these troubled times. We will continue to have stressful times in our lives but now I can slide through them. I am able to hike all over the Utah mountains and keep up with 8 grandkids. I mountain bike and ride side by sides almost all year long and feel great. I travel a lot as our parents live in different states, and flying or taking long drives no longer make me sick. I recently drove across the United States from Florida to Utah and felt fine when we were done. You will get there. I have confident that everyone of us can get well and survive this wicked virus.

Have you ever watched your house get full of dust and dirt, or your bathroom get dirty with hard water and filth from everyone washing their hands and taking a shower? Well believe it or not our brains can get a lot of this uncollected dirt just like our bodies and homes, cars and even our thinking. The journaling that I mentioned in the past will help with our overwhelming buildup of emotional anger, bitterness and hatred that we have towards other people.

Whenever my feelings were all too overwhelming for me to handle because of emotional upset from another person, I would either get my journal out or grab a piece of paper or notebook. It would depend on what I was going to do with it in the future. I would start jotting down every thought about this person whether it be good or bad, and to every detail on how the hurt or affected me. One time I wrote 19 pages of my feelings on a notepad. As I wrote it my anger flared up and I was not nice to this person on paper. But I did get it out of my head and on something that I could destroy. After I was done writing, I took it out into my back yard and set fire to it. Wow what an empowering feeling to get it out of my head. I would watch it go up in the smoke and allow the heavens and God to deal with it now. It was no longer mine to keep. My brain was now free. I repeat this concept because it is so important to keep our brains clear of debris and garbage. This happens to us on a weekly basis, so if it has to be a weekly ritual then so be it.

I went to a seminar to learn how to retrain the brain and let go of negative emotions and our mentor told us of an exercise he started to do in which every morning at 4:00 a.m. He would put his boots on and head out to his yard and move 12 rocks from his back yard to the front yard and the next night would do the same but move them from the front yard to the back yard. He continued to do this and every time he would ask himself, "now why are we doing this again?" He would reply back to himself because "I said so." This is a great exercise in discipline, detail and determination. It reminds me of the Dalai Lama and how disciplined he is in everything he does throughout his days.

If you have some deep emotional issues which I am sure a lot of us do, please seek some professional help. I mentioned EMDR previously in my chapter of forgiveness. Please consider this another great healing therapy in clearing the brain. This amazing therapy can help you clear out the deep rooted weeds. We all have them.

Another great healing modality is music. Music can touch people in a way that nothing else can. My husband and I play in a rock and roll band and simply have a blast and bless other lives with our music. We get the whole family involved and sing some great rock and roll songs from the Beatles and Coldplay, etc. My husband has written a lot of his own songs, so we also do a lot of his originals. I have seen a lot of wet eyes in the audience when he sings because his voice has such a way of touching the soul so deeply. I know that there have been so many bands turn to spiritual music and the words can be so emotionally breathtaking.

Everyone in this world is looking for some kind of HOPE, and music can be that very tool to deliver the hope you are looking for not only in the music but also the words. I can tell you of so many songs that I have heard that have choked me up and brought tears to my eyes because of the positive hope I feel of moving forward. Let's face it—this world is becoming very wicked and full of so much crime and violence that all of us at some point look forward to a great concert and dancing. So by all means turn up the music and dance. Every time I hear Bruno Mars and the wedding song "Marry You," I just can't sit still and want to dance. All the videos of different individuals using this song as a way to get engaged makes me so happy and want to dance. Not only does it represent something exciting, but it just sounds happy and fun, even if they are just looking for something dumb to do for one night. The next morning if they want to break up then that's coooooool. He won't blame youuuuuuu. Still sounds fun to me.

Reading great positive books and watching great movies are also so uplifting. I mean come on, who doesn't want to watch a happy love story with a positive ending. Also, there are many good self-help books that really help you think and bring some good positivity in your life. They can also teach us how to forgive and move on. I could suggest so many great books that I have read, but there are just too many of them to count. I really have a lot of favorites, but I must tell you the best book that I have in my possession was the Bible. We are living in times that are similar to the biblical times and I find it so fascinating and helpful. You will have to decide what is going to work for you, but I highly suggest reading at least 2 paragraphs of a good helpful book a day.

One of my favorite books was about a graphic design artist who made a living drawing illustrations for all types of books, but it wasn't easy getting to where he is today as he also had a chronic illness in which they prepared his mother that the illness would eventually take his life. After sitting in a hospital room with 5 other little boys that were slowly dying off, he decided to take a hold of his life and stop the process. They were in a hospital room and the one closest to the door would eventually die. After three had passed on, this young man looked at the last young man and said "I don't want to die." From that day forward he made a decision not to die. He would visualize in his mind that fighter jets were shooting bombs at his disease and blasting the enemy which was in his blood stream. This young boy continued this exercise continuously every day for hours. One day the doctors came to his mother and told her that her son was well and could go home. Can you imagine that? Such great hope the mind and determination can give us.

Self-care in our condition is as we all know very important, so please take time for yourself. Meditation is a great modality in healing the brain and teaching us to take time for ourselves. It teaches us how to breath and focus on staying calm at all times. Flying can be a scary moment that may last for hours, but meditation during a flight can help us get through that scary time. The military are taught to breath during attacks and times when the enemy is very close. We might not have situations like this in our life, but we do have close encounters of scary times. Traffic accidents and losing a loved one is very scary, and the grieving time can be scary as well. If you do have a loved one that has passed on, please understand that you can take as long as you need to grieve. It is very important to allow yourself the time you need during this grieving process.

There are 5 different steps and levels of grieving. They are denial, anger, bargaining, depression, and acceptance. They don't always run in this order and can jump around. Some might take longer to get through than the other ones. Allow yourself to go through each one of these. Divorce can bring on a grieving process, as well as a loss of a pet or loss of a job that you have had for years. There is no time limit to recover. When I was laid off from the job as animal technician in which I rehabbed pets back to normal, it did take some time to recover. I spoke about this also in my chapter of forgiveness. Because it was such a rewarding job and I felt like these little fur babies needed my help, it was like losing my family.  It was very rewarding and I loved it, but it was like going through a grieving process and did take some time as well as getting some EMDR therapy. It was rough but I did make it after a few years.

Life is going to be stressful and we are going to be faced with a lot of challenges. But we do have a lot of great tools now. When I first contacted this virus 35 years ago, I just knew I was dying and there was no hope. Now there are so many great modalities and tools that can help us in ways we never knew were possible. Also, we all have the most important subjects of all times on our side and in our court. Those are our brain and minds. Your brain can make you just as sick as it can make you well. We have so much information out there that can teach us how to use it.

Might I just mention another excellent book that teaches us that what we put out into the universe is what we will get back ten-fold. The Law of Attraction. This also applies to the friends we choose to hang out with. We always want to have friends that will benefit us and when we are with them, we want to feel like we want to always be with them. I have a friend like that. We may not share the same color of skin but we are true sisters from a different mother. She lifts me in every way and teaches me about forgiveness and lifts me in ways that most of my friends don't have any clue how to. She has had a lot of tragedy in her life, including losing a husband to a horrible gun accident while she was giving birth to their twin babies and thus was not able to attend her husband's funeral. She could definitely hold onto a lot of horrible events people have done to her, but she chooses to live happy, full of love and forgiveness and to move forward. We will always be connected at the hip. Whenever I need some uplifting time I call her and we will speak for hours. She did move to another state, but we still talk all the time.

What about just plain old laughing? Believe it or not, laughing is a wonderful exercise. Not only are you breathing excellently, but you are exercising your heart and lungs, increasing circulation and increasing your endorphins. Again, who doesn't want a rise of your endorphins? Just another boost to your immune system again naturally. One of my favorite funny movies that I love to watch if I want a good laugh is, and now don't think I am dumb, "Napoleon Dynamite." The first time I watched this show, I thought, "well this is the dumbest but funniest show I have watched in a very long time." I have watched other shows that make me laugh, but let's be real, this show has got some of the driest humor and I think that's what makes it funny.

Watching little puppies or kittens or even children play can be about the funniest event to just make your day. My grandchildren love to watch Funniest Home Videos. There is an endless number to them and we get such a kick out of people doing the dumbest things. Some of them I will admit looks like they could have really injured themselves. So plug in some good movies or videos and start to laugh and start to heal.

AGAIN, please get help if you have ever suffered a serious trauma and or tragedy that you are having a really difficult time with and not able to move on. A lot of these tragedies will bring on chronic illness's such as Epstein-Barr Virus syndrome. The stress can just be too much but there is help, and I have hopefully outlined a lot of the help that you will need to overcome this dreadful disease. You can get better. I got better with all of my tools and support group. It takes a whole team to win the game and you can do it. You will get better I promise, maybe not in your time frame but God's time frame. We are all rocks getting polished to become gems that

God is making out of us, and when we get it right we will shine.

***"Make time for the quiet moments, as God whispers and the world is loud."***

***"Love bears all things, believes all things, endures all things, hopes all things…Love never fails."***

# Chapter 11

# JUST HOW IMPORTANT ARE YOUR MOUTH AND TEETH?

This will be a short chapter although this is a subject that could take up a whole book by itself. I have seen books specifically just on the toxins in our mouth and the importance of oral care.

Part of one of my many jobs as a care giver is I run and operate an Air B&B out of my home for people who come to Utah for dental surgery at a homeopathic dental office just up the street from where I live. These patients come from all over the United States seeking some type of hope for symptoms they have been suffering with for years. Symptoms that involve Epstein-Barr Virus, Lymes disease, Cytomegalovirus, and the list could go on forever.

I once had a dentist tell me that the mouth is the portal of all well-being throughout your body. I honestly believe that with words and food, this could very well be. The articles and food that we present to our body through our mouths could be the very thing that is destroying our lives.

Mercury has been labeled a toxin as well that our dentists used to use as a filling when we would get a cavity and have it drilled out. Dentists no longer use this metal as a filling. Now they are using a type of a porcelain filling which seems to be more suitable for fillings and won't poison our systems. So many sufferers with EBV are now looking into their mouth as a possible source of feeding the virus. I can tell you that people are swarming to the dentists to have their mercury removed out of their teeth. The new fillings that are white and being put into their place seem to be doing a great job. Both our boys had their teeth filled with porcelain and are doing great.

So now we have a new term in the dentistry business called cavitations that has now been bought to the medical field by dentists. It is not a new term in the medical field but is fairly new to dentistry. This is a formation of an empty space within a solid object or body. In other words, patients are now having cavitations formed between the bone and teeth that are filling up with infection and of course debris from food. Long term infection can also affect your immune system. The lymph system is trying to filter out the infectious cells and eventually it will get exhausted. Long term infection has also been known to cause and weaken valves in our hearts and our whole respiratory system. Eventually your sinuses also get plugged with no future in sight of ever being able to breath correctly. The drainage from that then makes its way to your respiratory system. UGHHHHHHHHHH.

When I was a youth about 13 and wanting to play sports, I had to have a physical in order to play. The doctor detected a heart murmur in one of my pulmonary valves. At the time I had had numerous sore throats and as he examined my mouth and tonsils discovered I had a lot of infection on my tonsils in which I obviously had onsillitis as well. He told me this was the reason that I had developed a heart murmur. He prescribed antibiotics immediately and I did take the full prescription. Over a number of years, the heart murmur cleared up and I eventually grew out of it. I never did have my tonsils removed but later both of our boys would have theirs removed as well as their adenoids.

The patients that I take care of at my Air B&B after dental surgeries are having that very surgery on their mouth in removing infection and dead tissue that has collected over years in their cavitations. I have seen a lot of these patients feel much better in the recovery room having just had the surgery done. They do feel like they are on the right path to getting rid of any toxins that might be poisoning their body and depleting their immune system. I think that having a good dentist and oral surgeon with your team of healing team members, and keeping track of your teeth and gums are both extremely important. I'm not saying go out and have your cavitations cleaned because this would have to be diagnosed by a good oral surgeon and a good dentist.

There are obviously a lot of hidden bacteria and toxins hiding in our teeth and gums that we have no idea are there. A lot of times it can be from the air that we breath. Here in Utah where we live, we have many oil refineries which excrete a lot of pollutants into the air on top of the automobile exhaust. That is simply a disaster waiting to happen and we are breathing in this air. There will be times when the air is so full of garbage that is will look like we just had a dust storm. Actually, it would be better if we had a windstorm as it would blow all the garbage away.

That's why it is so important for oral care. I remember going in for a physical at the age of 55 and my doctor who happens to be a female doctor that I really like, said don't forget to brush twice daily and floss daily. I mean here I am a grown woman and grandmother being told to remember to brush. As my mother is aging now I realized that she has to be reminded to brush her teeth and of course floss as well.

Getting root canals now, dentists have decided, are starting to cause problems with that particular tooth. I once had a tooth that had gone bad, and in my estimation had developed severe nerve damage. It was so painful and I saw no relief in sight after a set of antibiotics. It did have a crown on it and I was told that I could get a root canal over the top of the crown. I was sitting in a chair at a dentist office getting ready to receive a root canal and at the last minute changed my mind.

He called my family dentist and away I went to get it pulled. I was in such excruciating pain from this tooth that I was shaking. My dentist was so sweet and they covered me with blankets and took their time pulling the tooth. He did insert synthetic bone to get me ready for a possible implant. Later down the road I chose a bridge to be placed instead and I am glad I made that decision.

It took several months to recover from this and a year before I had the bridge put in its place. I would have nerve pain for several months and still to this day, every once in a while, I feel like I have phantom tooth with pain. I know most of you know what I am talking about. I am very glad that I didn't have an implant put in its place as I believe it would have to have been removed eventually.

When I had my gallbladder removed, no one could have prepared me in experiencing what is now called phantom pain where it used to be. I also believe that is again what stirred up my hypoglycemia. Whenever you have an organ removed it puts added extra stress on the surrounding organs. I found that out the hard way. Again, I wished I had known what I know now. I maybe could have saved my gallbladder and a lot of added extra stress on my surrounding organs. The last MRI I had showed that I have developed a fatty liver. The doctor asked me if I was a heavy drinker. I laughed and said absolutely not. I believe that my liver has become taxed and stressed because of the virus and having my gallbladder removed. I also believe that a lot of sufferers have fatty livers because it is a way for our liver to protect itself. If you think about what they call mono, it is sometimes referred to as the liver fever sickness. I got off of the subject of root canals but felt like I wanted to share that about the liver.

Apparently what happens is during the root canal, as your tooth is being drilled into and wires and whatever are being placed, bacteria also makes its way into the root of the tooth which can sit for years and fester. Eventually it turns abscessed. Once you hit that situation, the pain can be very unbearable.

If you eat a lot of sweets and or foods high in acids, this can severely break down the enamel on your teeth. The tooth becomes decayed and eventually can fall out or have to be pulled. This is also why it is so important to brush twice a day and especially at night before you go to bed to remove any food particles that would soon turn into bacteria and start to cause infection.

In my own studies with my own body, I have realized that when I brush my teeth right before bed and even gargle with some good antiseptic mouth rinse that kills germs that cause plaque and gingivitis and bad breath, my stomach isn't as acidy in the morning. If you think about it of course that makes sense. After all, your saliva and digestive enzymes start to work immediately whenever you put food in your mouth.

When there is no food, there is no digestion taking place and your stomach acids can take a little bit of a break.

When I was at my worse and basically homebound, I would have to go stay with my grandmother as I could not be left alone at all. She was the one who would take me to all of my appointments when I was at my wits end with symptoms and no explanation as to what I had. She would always comment about my breath being so horrible, probably because at the time I was dying inside or so that's what I literally felt like was happening. I think now looking back on my situation, I believe I was dying on the inside. After all there was a virus that was trying to take over and killing off my insides, so no wonder if it was because all the cells in my body were in fact being destroyed. I now brush sometimes three times a day and keep mouthwash with me at all times. This is so, so, so important with sufferers of EBV.

One other little bit of information I have again discovered within myself as I begin to heal is what comes out of my mouth. Everyone loves to cuss, RIGHT? Let's face it—you do feel much better after you have just thrown out one of those blasted 4-letter words and now you have shown and conquered your opinion as well as letting people you know just how mad you really are. Well not quite. So what has happened is you have raised all the bad chemicals in your brain and started a chemical war in your body. Our bodies are constantly trying to fight for a homeostasis balance. This is exactly what it is, a balance of every single chemical and hormone that is made in your body. When we cuss and lose our cool it raises it raises our cortisol and aldosterone. This is an overload of adrenaline which is not what we need right now. So when that takes place our bodies are working really hard to bring down those chemicals and it puts a strain and overload on our brain to raise our dopamine and norepinephrine to bring our body back into homeostasis. Another blast of unwanted stress and work for our bodies.

So for me, I try and look at everything with compassion and love. I know you have always heard the term "don't judge until you have walked in their shoes for a while." This I believe to be very true. Everyone has trials of some sort they are working through and dealing with. Everyone has a story of some sort or another. If ever anyone tells you differently then they are not being truthful. We are all dealing with some sort of stressful challenge in our lives. So we should stop and count to 10 before letting the old cuss words fly. When I get to points in my life like this, I just throw on my walking shoes and take a walk. This seems to help with frustration, and anytime I can be outside, I do feel the healing power of mother nature.

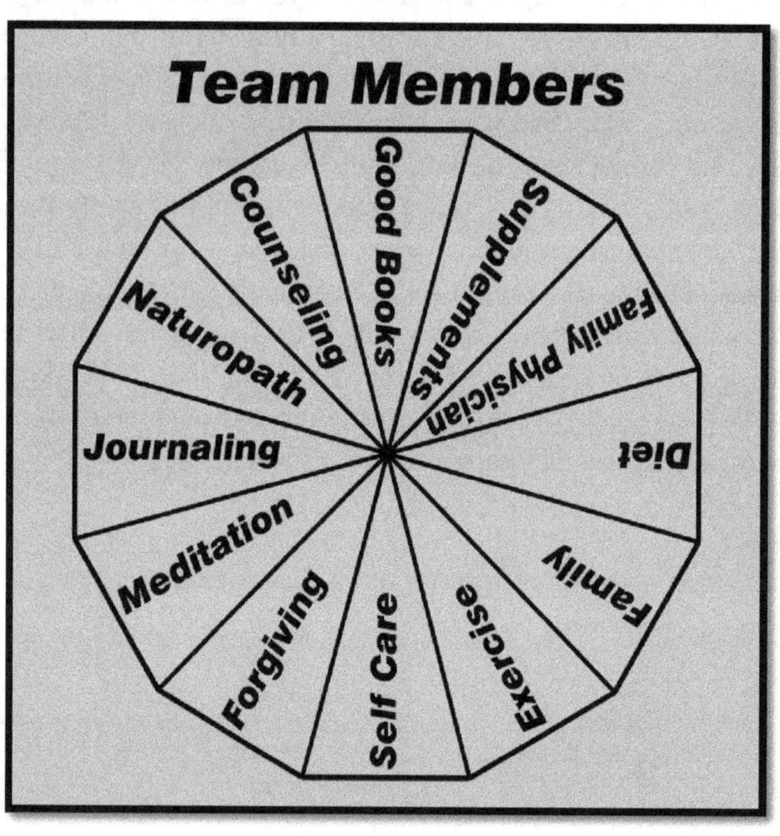
Team Members
Good Books
Supplements
Family Physician
Diet
Family
Exercise
Self Care
Forgiving
Meditation
Journaling
Naturopath
Counseling

# Chapter 12

# DON'T BLOW IT

Once you start to feel a little like a normal person, this is such a critical time. I always like to remember what I call the 5-Ds. I will number them and explain to you how important they are and why we should implement them in our life.

1. **Desire:** A strong feeling of wanting something to have or wishing for something to happen. The first desire that we all yearn for is to get well and we all are wishing that it would happen immediately. Unfortunately, this does take some time and there is no quick fix for this little virus. The first decision we need to make is the Desire to get well. Once this has been made then the next step is:

2. **Determination:** Firmness of purpose. Once you have established the Desire, then being determined to get better is the next step. Almost like an addict but not quite. If you can develop Determination you have already got your mind set in the right place. The next step is:

3. **Dedication:** The quality of being dedicated or committed to a task or purpose. This is almost like being in a marriage or starting a new job. No matter

the pay or the ups or downs, which are going to happen, you are still dedicated and committed in moving forward fighting for what you believe in, like getting well, or what you consider is a perfect goal. Getting better in my book is a great goal and if you put your mind to anything in this life, you will accomplish. Faith is amazing and can move mountains if you want it to. The next step is:

4. **Discipline:** The practice of training people to obey rules or code of behavior. We do have laws in our country and we have to obey them or we can go to jail or prison and then our free agency has been taken from us. Discipline with a virus is a lot similar in the fact that if we waiver with our plan and/or our recipe for getting well, we might have a mess on our hands or a relapse. And can I tell you that as a survivor, I don't ever want to go through another relapse ever again. I am willing to obey any recipe and follow the guidelines that I have to in order to stay well. So if I have to avoid cake and ice cream at a birthday party then so be it. At least I will wake up the next morning feeling good again and not like I just pulled off a good drunk or something to that affect and now have a hangover. The next step is:

5. **Detail:** Individual feature, fact or item. So this is exactly what it means. We must be detailed in all that we do. We can't just say, "well I ate a good lunch so I don't have to eat anything that good for dinner." WRONG.. You have to be detailed in your supplements, diet, exercise and your lifestyle change.

> You can't just pick and choose a few items you want to do to get well, it has to be the whole plan. There are 13 items in the pie to getting well and you can't leave one out and think you will get better. You might start to get better but sooner or later without the whole pie in place as your team, you probably will start to waiver a little or maybe even have a full-blown reactivation. I tried to do this once on my own and found out that I have to stick very strictly to the plan with my team players. Your team players are all necessarily people. They can be a lot of different healing modalities that I have discussed as well.

So remember when you are not in training, your opponent is and the opponent is the virus. We have to be on our toes at all time. There is no quick or easy fix and this virus will take a lot of time, patience, love and understanding. You will get to know your body and your mind in a way that you never knew. This will be a time to reflect and bring together a complete lifestyle change and most likely a permanent life change. Your mind will be the most important attribute to your well-being. Believe it or not psychological and spiritual development are both capable of reversing the disease process. The disease can unleash a self-discovery, and the virus can in turn attack a rebellious immune system. By now the victim has been reborn and can reject the old self and its disease. When a person with EBV makes a positive personality change thoroughly, the body's defense may now eliminate the disease, which is now part of the new self.

Once you have discovered the recipe for getting well it is so important that you don't fall into bad habits and think that now you are healed you can start to get back to your old self. That is just not going to happen.

The time is now to start to enjoy life. Get outside and enjoy the majestic beauty of the world. Sit in the sunshine for as long as you can with your face facing that warmth shining down on your body and face warming it up like sitting by a natural heater—only this heater also puts off a lot of vitamin D.

There are so many magnificent beauties that God created for our use. The beautiful mountains, white powdered beaches with mesmerizing sounds of the ocean's waves, streams and rivers with the meditating sound of running water, lakes with stunning colors of clear blue water, flowers that beautify are simply indescribable, canyons and rock formations that take your breath away and make you feel like you are on a different planet. This world is so full of healing power with the plants and trees. The oxygen that these wonderful living organisms put off are extremely healing and should be included in our daily activity.

One of my favorite past times is to camp and enjoy the beauties of the outdoors. If you feel well enough and are up for the task of a nice hike, get started and enjoy yourself. Try not to over- do yourself as to wake up the next day feeling like you just got hit with a truck. When I get ready, I always feel like I have just had a reset to my battery.

We also have our three little fur babies by our sides at all times. I grew up with animals my whole life. My Grandpa was a veterinarian and so we have always had indoor 4-legged family members live with us. They are just about the cutest most precious therapeutic little members of our healing process. Most people that can afford and accommodate an extra fury member in their family usually go out and find that special little creature. They are so loving unconditionally and happy to see you when you get home from work or even just the store after you have been gone a whole 20 minutes. Now we can get therapy permits for our fury family members so they can travel with us for free.

I worked at a veterinarian clinic in which I worked with a lot of service pets and therapy pets for all types of clients who suffered either from PTSD or war veterans returning home from the wars. I can't even describe the wonderful stories I witnessed from having a pet. I have had both kitty cats and dogs. They all have a special place in our home and lives.

Massages are extremely therapeutic and once you feel like you can tolerate one, please treat yourself to a full body. Remember to tell your therapist to back off on the pressure as you are just here for relaxation and trying to heal a pulled muscle. As a therapist myself and instructor at a massage school, you have to be specific on your needs and wants. A nice Swedish is just what the doctor ordered for a relaxing evening and a good night's sleep.

Remember mind over matter and slow and easy does it. If you have ever had a hangover from a fun night out with your friends and wished you had never started to drink because the next day you can't move or even stand, think about that for a long time and also think about how many times you told yourself you never ever want to do that again until the next time it happens again. Well I must ask you one question, "did you not learn your lesson from the last time you did this?" That is what the same concept is of getting well from this dreadful virus.

Take time to develop some hidden talents you might have. I took time to learn to play the piano. I have always wanted to play a musical instrument and I love the way the piano sounds, so I took lessons. It wasn't very easy at first because there were days that I just didn't feel good enough to go to my lesson but I forced myself. From there I started to play percussion instruments and the drums. I find joy in creating music and with our band playing and entertaining the public, I can now share those talents. Write a song or poem about your journey through this healing time. Sometimes just being a good listener can be very rewarding and helps someone in need. There are numerous volunteer jobs you can get involved in, but again remember to take it slow.

I have learned to love my fellow man in such an extraordinary way as I continue to heal. I have become more in tune to people's disabilities and needs. I have developed a deep compassion for humankind as everyone has problems and everyone is suffering from some sort of malady. If anyone tells you otherwise then they are lying. None of us are exempt from trials as God is molding us into the courageous warriors he knows we are all capable of being. I loved this saying I found in one of my favorite books. "God will not have his work made manifest by cowards. A man is relieved when he has put his heart into his work and done his best".

I start my day off with gratitude and showing how grateful I am by always serving someone throughout the day. It can be holding a door open for a stranger, listening to someone in need, taking over a treat to someone who has been having a rough day. It can be taking your pet for a walk or giving someone a ride whose car just broke down. There are so many ways to serve your fellowman and get out of your own sufferings and difficulties. I would always forget how bad I hurt or felt like I had just been hit with a truck when I would find ways to serve. Ask your church leaders if there is an elderly person that likes to be read to or just would like a visit. The elderly get so lonesome being cooped up in their home all day with no one to visit. There are many ways to serve and show gratitude. This believe it or not can be another exercise in healing. It is tough at first because you can barely take care of yourself, but I promise you will forget all your worries.

Be grateful for this opportunity to grow and hopefully share your experience with other sufferers. I am grateful for a new day to create positivity in the world. I am grateful for being alive now and without pain and having my brain back. I am grateful I can run and walk without feeling like I have to go to bed. I am grateful I can play with my 8 grandkids. I am grateful I can travel and feel like a normal person finally. You all will get there. I love all you tons that are suffering with this nightmare wicked virus. Your dream will eventually come true.

Praying and giving thanks and talking with God should be part of your healing plan and daily routine. I am sure a lot of you have had a prayer in your heart for every second and minute of the day just to get you through. But as you continue to see better days and soon weeks and months, never forget to give thanks to our maker. God is simply taking stones and polishing them into beautiful Gems.

> ***"MAKE TIME FOR THE QUIET MOMENTS AS GOD WHISPERS AND THE WORLD IS LOUD."***
>
> —Author unknown

You will get better over time. You have a great team with great support. Your teammates are cheering you on and expect you to make first place in the fight for winning the battle with Epstein-Barr Virus.

I have outlined a pretty simple plan with diet and exercise and supplements to beat and conquer this virus and to become a better person once and for all. I pray all of you reading this book will find some sort of comfort and relief knowing you are not alone and that there are other sufferers like you. You will get better and I bless and pray for all of you on your journey to Recovery.

* * * * *

If you have any questions or comments regarding the contents of this book, please email me at:

tristinabown@gmail.com

CPSIA information can be obtained
at www.ICGtesting.com
Printed in the USA
LVHW080845090421
683790LV00001B/1